I Want More of
Everything

I Want More of
Everything

Eda LeShan

Newmarket Press
New York

94 95 96   10 9 8 7 6 5 4 3 2 1

Library of Congress Cataloging-in-Publication Data
LeShan, Eda
I want more of everything/Eda LeShan.— 1st ed.
p. cm.
ISBN 1-55704-211-X
1. Self-actualization (Psychology) in old age. 2. Life change events in old age. 3. Adjustment (Psychology) in old age. 4. LeShan, Eda. I. Title.
BF724.85.S45L47   1994
155.67—dc20   94-22544
CIP

Quantity Purchases
Companies, professional groups, clubs, and other organizations may qualify for special terms when ordering quantities of this title. For information, write Special Sales Department, Newmarket Press, 18 East 48th Street, New York, N.Y. 10017, or call 212-832-3575.

Book design by MaryJane DiMassi

Manufactured in the United States of America

First Edition

This book is lovingly dedicated to my parents, Max and Jean Schick Grossman, for giving me extraordinary roots, and to my husband, Larry, for giving me wings. When I wrote my first book, Larry made me change my library-card listing from "psychologist" to "author," and here I am about twenty-five books later.

Acknowledgments

Special thanks and loving wishes to those who helped me the most with this undertaking: Keith Hollaman, Helen O'Donahue, Ginger Rothé, AnneMarie Simone, and Phyllis Wender. With special gratitude to the readers of my *Newsday* column for keeping me alert and feeling cared for.

Much of the material in this book comes from the weekly column I write in the New York newspaper *Newsday*. The column is the most fun undertaking I have ever had in my writing experience. People sometimes ask how I can still think of topics after four years, fifty-two columns a year. It's easy; at least ten things happen to me every day that have to do with my being in my seventh decade. I hope what I observe about my own life may be helpful to others, both men and women. While there are marked differences in how we feel and act, men and women share much in common—and perhaps need to do so even more. The human condition belongs to all of us—pain and pleasure, hope and despair, grief and joy. The human condition also means that men and women together can strive for more fulfillment in the later years.

Contents

VII
EMOTIONAL HANG-UPS

VIII
HARD TIMES

IX
LOOKING AHEAD

Bliss

In the middle of the night,
My bedroom washed in moonlight
And outside
The faint hush-hushing
Of an ebbing tide,
I see Venus
Close to
The waning moon.
I hear the bubbling hoot
Of a playful owl.
Pierrot's purrs
Ripple under my hand,
And all this is bathed
In the scent of roses
By my bed
Where there are always
Books and flowers.

In the middle of the night
The bliss of being alive!

May Sarton
12–15 October 1991

I Want More of
Everything

I Want More of Everything!

THE WINTER OF 1994 WILL PROBABLY BE REMEM-
bered by most people as the year of the big (and end-
less!) blizzards. Quite properly so, but I will remember
it most of all as the winter in which I signed a contract
for a year's option for an off-Broadway production of a
play I had written. I have no idea whether it will actually
be produced, but the option represents a major turning
point in my life.

When I was a child I created plays for the entertainment of my parents' friends at dinner parties. I wrote,
directed, and acted in these productions; my younger
brother acted and did what I told him to do—excellent
training for my becoming a stage director. At a summer-
camp play a Hollywood agent, visiting friends, told my
father I had "histrionic ability." I didn't know what that
meant, but knew it was something good. At the age of
seventeen, I played two parts in a famous anti-war play,
Bury the Dead, by none other than Irwin Shaw, and most
of the audience didn't know I was playing two different
parts. And so I became a nursery-school teacher, of
course!

I was a nice kid and loved my parents. My father especially felt that the theater was a nice hobby, but too unreliable as a profession; most fathers of most girls in "my day" strongly urged us to become teachers. Actually, my father was very advanced in his thinking—one of the few men of his generation who wanted his daughter to have a career in addition to marriage and parenthood.

Teaching, he said, would give me security, a pension. I am glad he was too old to notice when this formula ceased to exist.

I loved working in nursery schools, but I wanted more. I got degrees in education and psychology, worked with parents in child-study discussion groups, wrote several books about family life, spent three years as moderator of a television series, *How Do Your Children Grow?*, wrote books for children about feelings, and spent a great deal of time and money on psychotherapy because I saw that as the best way to understand more about myself and other children. My husband, Larry, and I traveled while we were still young. Each of us became "successful" in our work; parenthood enriched our lives. We both wanted as much of life as we could possibly experience, and the resulting adventure has lasted fifty years. What more could a person ask for?

All through my life going to the theater has been a special joy. I began to think, by the time I was forty or fifty, that if I had my life to live over, I would have insisted on studying the arts in college. Deep down, under the surface of a good and satisfying life, there was this gnawing sense of having missed something. I began fooling around with playwriting in my early sixties. I

wrote short one-act plays. Many of them were related
to Larry's work of helping cancer patients through psychotherapy. One play in particular was performed many
times at seminars and conferences and was eventually
taped for use with other groups.

At seventy-two I will become a professional play-
wright if the option on the play results in a production.
And the reason this has happened is that I could never
settle for what I had, I always wanted more. It is one
of the reasons I am still alive. I have had a mild stroke
and frequently feel unsteady; in addition, I've had a
slight heart attack. I am a weather reporter by virtue of
my arthritic pain. I could list several more unwelcome
signs of aging. Often when I sit down to write I may
spend half an hour trying to remember the next word
I need. (Most of the time I end up asking someone else
to help me.) But when I sit down to work on a play,
time stops, nothing hurts. At the end of a long day's
work I feel refreshed. Larry frequently cries when he
reads my plays. That's all the approval I need!

Why I am telling you all this in a book about growing
old, the sequel to *It's Better to Be Over the Hill Than
Under It*? Because it is my conviction that every breath
of life matters, and to have the fullest possible adventure
of living we need to understand that it is never too late
to continue the quest for more, More, MORE. I have
learned that too many people wither and die for lack of
divine discontent, which means waking up every morning with the firm intent of using every bit of talent and
skill and understanding to find new meanings, new
strengths.

The most important element in finding more is to

have a pure heart. More of everything for me means living more fully. It doesn't mean accomplishing anything for the approval of others. I will happily go on writing plays, even if not one ever sees the light of day. Wanting more everything has nothing to do with things, possessions, status, or pleasing others. The "everything" is what is in each of us that can make us more than we are at any given time. The "everything" is self-understanding; the "everything" is reaching inside, using the gifts that may lie dormant for a long time. The "everything" is the joy of fulfilling oneself. It is the fact that my pleasure is in writing and all else is gravy. And my message to you is that I hope you have more opportunities for self-fulfillment during these years of *growing* old. The operative word is growing. Never settling for where you are but always ready and willing for surprising yourself with your own gifts. Every day brings with it painful signs that physically I am rapidly falling apart, but what remains intact is an indomitable urge to live more fully.

Chances are that every child has dreams that were never fulfilled. Adults expected us to develop in certain ways; they had goals and expectations. In our general age group, few of our parents were saying, "Go out and find yourself," as many young parents, thank goodness, now are saying to their children. What were our secret dreams? What fantasies did we have that we were sure could never be fulfilled? Isn't it time to reexamine one's life, to find the unfinished wants and do something about them?

When I drive around the Cape Cod areas where more

than twenty years ago I could ride a bicycle five to ten miles a day, I feel nostalgic and a little sad. It occurs to me that not only will I never ride a bicycle again (because of arthritic knees and dizziness), but I will never run again, ever, for the rest of my life. To be young and healthy is an "everything" I cannot ask for. But now I have a cat I love so much I'd die for him. And I live in the country where I can look forward to spring flowers. I swim three times a week in a beautifully heated indoor pool. I enjoy classical music more than I ever have. I can sit at my desk and write plays. Too many people in their seventies (sometimes even in their twenties, thirties, or forties) think that nothing new can happen to them; they are settled in their world. To me that is like burying oneself in concrete while still alive and breathing. For me each day is different. Some of what happens will be good, some bad. Some news will be joyful, some painful. But whatever happens, I know I won't stop in my tracks and say, "That's IT, folks." Who can tell what new discoveries I will make about myself. How exciting!

It may seem as if this book, a new collection of commentaries for older people, mostly drawn from my weekly columns in *Newsday*, is focused on the problems of getting old. I see no advantage in the denial of reality. But that is never the whole story. The only way in which we can be permanently crippled by the fact of aging is if we should ever stop wanting more out of life. It is never too late for growing and changing. It is always possible to discover deeper wellsprings of self-discovery. No human being ever uses up all he or she can be. Now is our time to continue this quest.

I

How to Feel Young in an Aging Body

Staying Young or *Feeling* Young?

I DO NOT BELIEVE THAT WE CAN WASTE TIME STRUG-gling to deny that we are getting older all the time. I believe all one's energy must be focused on as good health as possible and a full and meaningful life.

The secret of staying young in an aging body is simple. It's a four-letter word: RISK.

I know quite a lot about this. Among other personal experiences, I have been through a major crisis which has been my "research" on this matter of risk. For four years my husband and I had what seemed to be the ideal arrangement for our needs. He had (and still has) an office-apartment in Manhattan. I had an office-apartment in Riverdale (the West Bronx) with an absolutely mag-nificent view of the Hudson River and the cliffs of the Palisades. The George Washington Bridge lit up with green lights at night seemed a strange wonderland. Twenty-three floors above the sailboats and yachts, what a place to meditate and write! But gradually this setting seemed to become too remote from the earth, too high up in the clouds; I began to feel that for the final decades of my life I needed to be closer to the earth, right there with the trees, flowers, birds and ducks, not gazing down from a great height.

We bought a house on Cape Cod—the place I love the most, close to my granddaughter, with a yardful of birds and woods to walk in. I did this before selling my office-apartment—a terrible, terrible financial hazard. I made the distance between myself and my husband much more difficult for commuting, and I saddled us with a horrendous mortgage. My husband, who surely understands risk-taking (I suppose it is our mutual religion), went along for one irrational crazy reason. A play of mine was produced quite far off-Broadway— North Carolina* to be exact!—and I knew I wanted to spend whatever is left of my life writing plays (most of the time).

I know from personal experience and from so many of the letters I receive that feeling depressed about the realistic changes in one's life can be alleviated, if not totally cured, by concerning oneself with others and by bringing new meaning into one's life. Feeling better often starts with getting rid of things we cannot change, including old relationships that make us feel only bitter and full of self-pity. One wise lady wrote me, "I was deeply hurt that a niece I had helped a great deal seemed to be rejecting me. I had helped to pay for her college education; I'd given her a trip to Europe for her honeymoon; I'd babysat with her first child. Gradually I felt her withdrawing from me. I was hurt and angry. After a while I realized I was just hurting myself. A friend

---

*Add Georgia, Florida, Atlanta, and a few places in the Midwest, since!

told me about a young man who was struggling to go to college who had been blind from birth. He needed a loan to go to graduate school. I said I would help. Bob came to see me, we talked for a long time. We like the same things. He explained how he managed to study, to go to the theater, to sing in a church chorus. We became buddies. I feel good to be helping someone again."

There are, of course, more serious kinds of depression. If depression continues for a long time and increases one's anxiety, it is time to seek medical help. "Situational depressions" can be greatly helped by talking with a professional counselor. There are agencies in many communities that will send someone to one's home, if necessary. You can find out what resources there may be by calling your local council of social agencies or individuals or groups dealing with the issues of aging. Adjusting to getting old is a legitimately tough challenge for many people. But we don't have to take it lying down.

This book is, I know, disproportionately about women. I can only speak from that point of view, but happily I have gotten wonderful letters from men saying all the same issues and views apply to them. I think that's true, but my experience has suggested that, in most phases of living, women have had the edge as survivors. I hope that I and other women who love men can serve as role models.

In spite of certain strident voices of the past few decades I have, myself, never doubted for one moment that boys and girls, men and women, are different, and I hope it shall always be thus. Equal rights under the law does not mean "the same." As I get older I realize that differences become clearer among the aging. As a general rule women are able to make a better adjustment to illness, hospitalization, widowhood; they communicate their feelings more easily than men. Women tend to cry and wail that they can't possibly take care of themselves—and then they do just that. Women complain more and then feel better. Women make new friends in new places; men need help to make new connections. Women can stay longer in their own homes—cooking, shopping, cleaning, seeing and entertaining friends and relations. Men (with some exceptions) have not learned to take care of themselves. I think my widowed father was a fairly typical example; except for the meals I cooked for him, or the restaurants we took him to, he seemed to be living on cold cereal. Even those women who may have been catered to and protected from realistic chores seem to adapt to check-writing, shopping, paying bills, and hiring helpers more easily than men living alone. Needless to say, these generalities have many exceptions, but not enough to wipe out the observations.

Men have a harder time with retirement, partly, of course, because in our generation a man's work was paramount. Women have always assumed most responsibilities for keeping their households functioning, and when their career days may end, there are still the grandchildren. Women tend to have some real concerns about " 'til death do us part, but not for lunch." Neither men nor women do well with the issue of twenty-four-hours-a-day togetherness, but women tend to complain more openly and then feel better.

What I have observed too often to be accidental is that in general women are less paralyzed psychologically by getting old. We are survivors from way back. After all, it is women who give birth and then go on to nurture their children usually more intensely and responsibly than men. I see this important emotional distinction as an integral part of Nature's plan.

One of the skills for survival among women is mutuality of experiences. We love to share our miseries and joys. Who carries around more pictures of the grandchildren? Who talks more openly about a gall bladder operation or new dentures? I don't know any men who talk freely about a prostate operation—I have the feeling this is true even among themselves, although I admit that is merely an impression not backed up by personal knowledge. But my husband agrees men don't share as freely as women, especially about depression. In contrast, my friends and I are wont to start a telephone conversation by telling each other, "I'm going to kill myself." This declaration may occur because we have gained five pounds, have trouble bending because of arthritic knees, or haven't been able to find a suitable dress for a wedding.

When an older man retires or loses his job, he may not be able to talk about it, but his wife recognizes a deep depression when she sees her husband wearing a bathrobe all day, playing solitaire, and watching soap operas on TV. Getting old is no picnic for anyone. It inevitably raises the specter of mortality; it brings with it unexpected infirmities; it may scare us half to death financially. We all need as much help as we can get to use this time of our lives as creatively as possible. My hope is that when we women get things straight we can help men do likewise. As one sensible wife said, "Listen, Harry, if you can learn to *talk* to me now, after forty years of marriage, we might be able to walk into the sunset with a smile."

Women as Role Models for Men

I KNOW A WOMAN WHO WAS HER HUSBAND'S "LITTLE flower." He paid all the bills, gave her an allowance for food, went shopping with her for most of her clothes, and made all the arrangements when they traveled. When he recently died, her grief included a good deal of terror; how could she possibly survive on her own with no skills, either career or otherwise?

I met her a year after her husband died. She was working in a boutique four mornings a week. She had hired an accountant to help her with bills and taxes. Her house was on the market and she told me she was planning to move to a condominium designed for older people, which included some minimal medical care for emergencies. She had traveled on her own to visit a son who lived two thousand miles away. She said, "Of course, I miss Ralph terribly, but you know, I'm really enjoying shopping for my own clothes. I've even managed a couple of dinner parties for my close friends. I just signed up for a course in beginner's Spanish at the high school—I think it's important to at least know a little Spanish if you are going to live in Florida." When

I looked startled at her obvious independence and enjoyment of her life, she laughed, "You never know what you can do until you do it!"

When my father was widowed, he remained dependent on others to take care of him. He never initiated any activity on his own. He refused to consider joining a chess club or going to lectures at a nearby adult school. He needed, for the rest of his life, to depend on the kindness of women. If he ever cried, we never knew it; he seldom talked about my mother. It took effort on the part of his family to encourage him to see old friends.

Why were there such differences in response to widowhood? Why is it that women seem, on the whole, to deal with retirement, illness, and financial problems more successfully than men? Of course, basic personality differences play a part but gender is significant as well. Women tend to be survivors throughout their lifetime and, with some notable exceptions, of course, seem to deal more bravely and courageously with life changes.

In the future, differences of this kind may disappear as more boys are taught that it is okay to cry and to help with household chores and to see their fathers participating far more in cooking, doing laundry, shopping, and taking care of children. The next generation of old men may be a new breed. If one observes carefully in a supermarket there are very few old men alone, many more with wives, and scores of young men looking carefully at labels on packaged food as they wheel a baby in a shopping cart down the aisle.

The men of my generation often seem quite unprepared for functioning on their own. They buy new underwear when all their old shorts and shirts are dirty; they buy paper plates when the sink is overflowing with dirty dishes; they rarely plan ahead for social activities. They have limited skills in asking for help with problems they can't solve. They were simply unprepared to manage. The men who find they love being on their own are the exceptions.

For those of us with living husbands, education for survival should be seriously under way; for men alone and able to cope, children, friends, and relatives (probably mostly of the female persuasion!) need to help with guidance. We need to encourage the men we know who are alone to admit to vulnerability (that's been a woman's prerogative all along). Both individual and group therapy as well as support groups are important. Being alone need never be a sentence of misery and failure. Women seem more inclined to understand this fact and should serve as role models.

If Marilyn Monroe Had Grown Old

Can you imagine Marilyn Monroe sixty-eight years old? In anniversary recollections of her death thirty-one years ago, there were more than a few remarks about this fact. The focus has all been on youth and sex. But it has occurred to me that if she had lived long enough to have joined our senior citizen status, few would have paid much attention.

I remember exactly where we were on the day she died. We were crossing from Italy to France along the Mediterranean coast; stopping at the border town, we saw the black headlines in a French paper. I was naturally sorry that anyone so young had died, but I must confess Marilyn Monroe was not on my list of Very Important People. I never found her particularly sexy—and this was not only because I was a member of the same sex; my husband agreed that really sexy women were Simone Signoret or Sophia Loren, who were sensual women on the inside.

The intrigue about Monroe's life and death seems kind of excessive to me, almost bordering on the weird nonsense about whether Elvis is still alive. The worse the social-political picture becomes the more we love to turn to the inconsequential minutiae of life. I know I'm being a spoilsport, but homelessness and unemployment and the bestiality of the Serbs are of more central concern to me.

But with every television station, every radio program, every newspaper so often preoccupied with Marilyn, I can't help but notice. What I have been thinking about is how could a woman so loved, so unhappy, so torn by conflicting emotions, so used by so many men have grown into the kind of older woman I could have admired?

My idea of sexy, beautiful women who have aged like good wine are Katharine Hepburn and Jessica Tandy. Hepburn, more openly vulnerable, more able to be herself the older she gets, charms me out of my mind. The inner dignity and lovely romance of her now being able to tell the love story of her life seems to me to indicate a depth of passion which I doubt Monroe could have even imagined. And Tandy, with her wrinkles and white hair, is so beautiful she takes my breath away. And that long romance with Hume Cronyn only adds a bright luster to the fact that she remains a magnificent actress.

Any glamorous actress—or any aging woman for that matter—can look fifty at the age of seventy-five, with enough plastic surgery, facials, and makeup, but for us older ladies who haven't the money or the necessary masochism to follow suit, our role models have to be those women who are so alive, so focused on work and exuding a real sense of purpose, that physical appearance has to become a secondary concern.

Inner Beauty Can Last a Lifetime

ON ONE GERALDO RIVERA TELEVISION PROGRAM, there was great excitement on the part of the audience because the guests were going to demonstrate all the ways in which women could delay—even avoid—the appearance of getting old with all sorts of miracle creams, lotions, face-lifts, grotesque facial exercises, and vitamins. I turned it off when it got around to injecting various hormonal serums of sheep and an assortment of animal embryos.

It was now late afternoon at my house. I was wearing an old house dress and worn-out slippers. It has been, I guess, about thirty years since I had enough hair on my head to "style it." I had no makeup at the moment, and I remembered I should put in my upper denture— but my husband came home early. His endearments are none of your business, but it occurred to me that he is a brilliant man, not blind, that he loves the paintings of Monet so knows beauty when he sees it, and has a healthy and contemplative expression when he watches a young girl go by with a particularly charming behind.

How could he be glad to see me (as he has for forty-

nine years) when I look my age, have never used any
of the stuff produced by the vast youth products in-
dustries, and cannot recall one single moment of wishing
to be Miss America.

I figure that the ladies on Geraldo's program each had
to spend at least five hours a day (including weekends)
fighting the battle of aging so successfully. A good facial
alone takes at least an hour and a half, and shampoos,
makeup, pedicures, exercises, and consultations with all
the specialists must certainly fill up the day.

I began to wonder just how *I* might spend five hours
on any given day. Writing, studying, learning new things,
having new adventures, listening to my husband explain
some of his fascinating new research, watching birds and
ducks, planting flowers, laughing with aging friends
about our mutual aches and pains, swimming and walking and taking vitamins in acknowledgment of aging and
wanting to stay alive, sitting and thinking, going to the
theater and ballet and museums, meeting with young
parents and trying to help them understand their children better—good God, I have had a busy life! Almost
all of it internal—the enrichment and beautification of
my soul.

I know beyond a shadow of a doubt that I grow inside
me every day; I am wiser than I was ten years ago. I am
richer for experiences in living. Fortunately, I am told
by my most important admirer, "Your eyes are always
young. The face may age, but eyes, 'the windows of the
soul,' never need a facial."

Unless you catch me unawares in a supermarket or
on a beach, I do make some effort to maintain a rea-

sonably aesthetic public image. I take showers, have my clothes cleaned, maintain a wig or two. I wouldn't want to disgust or frighten anyone. But the main thing is I am nourished more than anyone has a right to expect, by love.

The wrinkles, the shaking cellulite, and the infirmities will surely increase. Even all those gorgeous ladies of sixty who look thirty-five will die someday. Each woman has a right to her own priorities, but I think I will have had a better run for my money.

Sue Me—I Like Being a Girl

IT WAS POURING; THE WIND WAS DOING AWFUL things to the "wind-chill factor." My husband, Larry, and I had to go to an office equipment store to have a Xerox machine fixed. The parking lot nearby was completely filled. Larry drove up to the door of the store, carried the Xerox machine inside, and told me to get out of the car and wait for him inside while he tried to find a parking space some distance away. I said, "No, no, you go inside, and I'll park the car. You're just getting over a cold." "Get out!" he yelled. "Don't argue with me!" Docile lamb that I am (??), I did as I was told. "Oh, thank you, Monsieur," I replied meekly.

Is he a chauvinist pig? Am I a weak and dependent female? No, to both questions. He just likes being a chivalrous man and I like being a girl. It is an old-fashioned attitude, I know. But I believe there is a big difference between chauvinism and chivalry. I learned this lesson about thirty years ago.

Larry and I were at a conference in Paris. One of the speakers was a brilliant scientist greatly respected by her colleagues. She was involved in fascinating research. She was also about four feet ten, wearing a frilly blouse, a short shirt, and high heels. She also had an adorable hat with imitation cherries on it. As we came out of the conference hall, we saw that it was pouring outside. Madam Hatem, *le docteur*, sighed: "Oh, dear," she said. "My new hat will be ruined!" My husband took off his jacket, held it over this little lady's head, and practically carried her to her taxi. When he returned, soaked to the skin, I said, "That was really brilliant, now you'll get pneumonia!" I added that I could get to the next taxi under my own steam. Larry wondered aloud if I would ever learn anything from that French lady. "I loved helping her," he said. "She made me feel nine feet tall."

Whenever I refuse a chivalrous offer, Larry says, "Oh, I see you didn't learn anything in Paris!" The truth is that I have led one of the most independent lives of any woman I know. I live alone some of the time; I have to my credit more than a few accomplishments, if I say so myself.

I can meet most crises, both minor and crucial, pretty well, when I have to. But I also love to feel protected— even infantilized. I love to feel this wonderful man wants to take care of me.

I read recently that a career woman was taking her boss to court for sexual harassment. He told her she looked pretty. I have an uncle who dared to tell a woman co-worker that her new dress was "a knockout" and who got a severe lecture about this "inappropriate remark." He added insult to injury by saying, "I'm so sorry, my wife likes me to comment on how she looks." "Well," this woman replied, "I guess your wife hasn't heard of equal rights for women." Equal? Does that mean "same"?

All revolutions tend to go to extremes for a while. I feel convinced that in the genuine and necessary struggle of women for equality in many areas of life where they have been powerless for too long, they have sometimes tended to throw the baby out with the bathwater. There are, thank goodness, genuine, certifiable differences between males and females—hormonal, neurological, psychological—and while I can understand (at least partially) that women may want to be firefighters and soldiers, as an old lady I want to say, "HOLD ON!" Some social customs, some attitudes are not necessarily chauvinistic; some feelings and behavior come from the whole idea of chivalry, which has actually been a civilizing force in the world. More chivalry taught to boys might slow down the awful epidemic of rape; fewer doors might be slammed in one's face; there might be generous and delighted offers of help at appropriate moments. It's fun, for heaven's sake! I love to watch the male swans and geese coming up behind Mama and the kids; they seem so proud of being protectors, ready for any emergency. My observations have led me to the conclusion that most mammals seem to accept and even enjoy a certain amount of specification as to differences. I like being a girl and Larry likes being a boy. We are equals in many ways (sorry, he's smarter than I am, but in this case I'm talking about genius; I do feel as capable and bright as most of the men I know). But when he acts as if I'm small and weak and in need of care, I love it.

Chivalry is not strictly a man-woman issue. I don't like it one bit when a woman in a hurry pushes me out of her way. I like it when a woman asks if she can help me to the car if I have a heavy bag of groceries. I suppose what it comes down to is that chivalry is compassionate interest in another human being, and while this has vast application to all human relationships, it especially delights me when the man I love wants to treat me in a way that isn't really necessary but makes me feel warm all over. What's so terrible about that?

II

THE CHANGING WORLD
AND ITS CHALLENGES

Progress Isn't All Wonderful

W E WENT TO VISIT A SMALL CITY WHERE I'D BEEN familiar with every street, where I had walked two to five miles a day and felt thoroughly at home. Twenty years later there isn't one single street or building that I could identify. Now there were at least fifteen new major highways around and throughout the city itself. The place where I had lived had been torn down about ten years ago and there were high-rise office buildings which made me think I was back in New York, somewhere around Madison or Lexington avenues on the East Side—one of the many places I have grown to hate; it is like being at the bottom of the Grand Canyon with a thousand honking horns.

I was devastated. There used to be beautiful gardens, lovely private homes, quiet neighborhoods that I remembered vividly. Instead, my husband and I drove in heavy traffic, trying desperately to escape, deciding to leave a day early if only we could find the airport. I hate it when nice small towns turn into noisy, confusing cities. I hate "Progress."

When we finally got home (the teeny-tiny airport of

my memory now looked like La Guardia Airport), it was a very hot day. I turned on the lights in my office, turned the air conditioner on, and thought for one terrible moment that I was going blind. All the lights were dimmer than ever before, because, my wiser husband explained, "There are now so many people, so many skyscrapers and enormous apartment buildings, that when the air conditioners are all going, in order to avoid another major blackout, the electric companies cut down on the current." Oh, where is Mr. Edison, who gave us light? It's going fast due to "Progress." I hate it.

No matter where I go—Massachusetts, Connecticut, North Carolina, and other countrysides—I search hungrily for the darling little birds I used to see in New Jersey and on Cape Cod. In the last three years I have seen two cardinals flying by. I search each summer for bobwhites and there aren't any. I can find plenty of Canada geese, grackles, crows, and starlings, the final survivors in the poisoned climate, in which tiny, delicate, little eggs can't survive the polluted water and air. Talk about "Silent Spring"! I would like to go back to before the Second World War, before nylons, before the wonderful world of chemistry. I hate the "Progress" that empties my life of delicate creatures.

My husband and I used to love to just get in a car and GO. There were always lovely new places to discover, beaches you could get to even through city streets; places you could find easily from the Post Road, and never any traffic anywhere we wanted to go except on Thanksgiving and Mother's Day. Now we stay home, we never drive anywhere if we can help it—the traffic is so confusing and dangerous; even the Merritt Parkway—our last hope of serene traveling—is being widened. We have given up cruise ships—too many people, too noisy, lousy food and entertainment even on what used to be the greatest ships. Plane travel in cattle cars is a nightmare, air fare beyond anything we could once have imagined. In my younger days I used to fly to Boston to "do" radio and TV publicity for the books I was writing. The air fare was sixteen dollars! Now even senior citizens pay about 190 dollars.

I also count every butterfly I see—now it's down to about one every other year. But in the midst of this complaining, my husband quietly mentions that I might not be overjoyed to have teeth pulled without novocaine, and outhouses don't thrill me at all, and an MRI study helped the doctor figure out where my stroke was, and my husband's life is being saved by heart drugs, and when I get around to cataract problems, lasers are a very nice thing—oh, well. That's how it goes. But at least I don't have to think progress is wonderful; it's just something I'm quite often glad to put up with.

The First Moon Settlers
Should Be Us

W HEN I LIVED IN NEW YORK I LIKED TO GO FOR a brisk walk almost every morning, except when the humidity and pollution level were intolerable. At six in the morning my route was quiet and ordinarily quite pleasant; there were not too many reminders that the planet earth is in danger. One day, however, I noticed that the crabgrass was winning a new war because the library I passed surely had no money for mowing the lawn, and the only birds I could see were those awful starlings, which have helped to wipe out the smaller birds weakened by environmental stress.

Last year as the Fourth of July was approaching, my adorable husband wanted to surprise me with a boat ride to watch the fireworks. He called every company in the New York harbor and couldn't find one which did not play loud rock-and-roll noise. (I will *not* call it music.)

There is hardly an hour of any given day when I don't have to acknowledge a sense of hopeless despair about the ways in which life has changed since we were young. All my contemporaries agree that despite the Depression and World War II we are now far more depressed about the future. If FDR were alive today and suggesting ways of helping all the disenfranchised people, nobody would back him up. Compassion and concern for one's fellow human beings seem so diminished in the city. Nobody really said a word when homeless people were removed from Columbus Circle in order for a restaurant (we have so few in Manhattan!) to be given the space. I keep searching for a sense of outrage about the social ills today, and I don't find it except among my own friends and the all too rare report of some person or community that has remained morally responsible.

What is this complaining all about? Simply that I think NASA should consider sending us old folks to be the first colony on the moon. We have had to become accustomed to change, most of which we don't like. I certainly feel I have become a stranger in my own land. It occurs to me that what with the traffic and the cost of medical care and fifty little kids in a class and television advertising, I might actually feel more at home on the moon. I don't think I paid close enough attention to *E.T.* or *Cocoon*. If I'd had a brain in my head I should have asked E.T. to take me along or gotten on *Cocoon's* ship. And one thing I feel relatively certain about— there would be no rock-and-roll on the moon.

What Happens to Rejected Children?

I WAKE UP ON A THOROUGHLY DISMAL DAY IN APRIL and turn on the radio news. The first story is about the two groups screaming and fighting outside an abortion clinic in Buffalo. The second story is about three teen-age boys setting fire to two homeless men asleep on a subway. A third story is about a high-school student being beaten to death by a gang. Am I the only person who sees the direct connection between these stories? I realize that the inevitable problems of getting older— what feels like the betrayal of one's body—is not half as serious or devastating as having to grow old in a terrible world in which I feel helpless.

I know quite a lot about children who were rejected at conception and forever after. I have met with them in prisons and on parole and in drug and alcohol reha- bilitation centers, and I know many of the teachers, social workers, therapists, and counselors who deal every day in heartbreak, too often in the hopeless re- alization that they cannot turn the tide of the wild rage of children and young people that pervades every aspect of our lives. The two groups yelling outside the abortion clinic speak on one side of unborn fetuses and on the other of women's rights, and I don't hear anybody talking about the psychological damage that would make children want to kill two old men or a young boy.

Among the many major issues we face, a population out of control tops the list. When the Bible was written and spoke of "being fruitful" there were one million people on the planet. Are we up to the trillions yet? It can't be long. When a scientist in a laboratory puts too many white rats in the same cage, they start killing each other; when there are more people on earth than can be tenderly loved and cared for, violence beyond our wildest imagination becomes an everyday reality.

My greatest concern in life as an old person is not arthritis or fatigue or a tendency to fall down, or to forget everything that's going on in the real world of names, faces, and words. I now realize I can live with and accept all that. What I cannot bear is what is happening to children—the lives of misery and despair so many live on this crowded and uncaring planet, and the people they grow up to be so filled with rage they all buy guns and knives to kill, or destroy themselves with drugs and alcohol to deaden the pain of living.

One of the worst experiences of my life was having a whole audience roar at me in fury when I said that *we* create the muggers, the murderers, the addicts, the society in which we live in terror, because of how we have neglected children. Like most people, that audience wanted blood and vengeance. The people on Death Row in any state in this country did not ask to be born crippled in mind or body. Go visit a hospital nursery in a poor neighborhood; the babies are just as cute as babies in fancy private hospitals but the majority are doomed to hunger, terrible danger, fear, and by three or four they know they should never have been born in such an unfriendly world.

The anti-abortionists better start visiting the ghettoes of this country and look at living children and decide what they want to do about *them.* Are they prepared to adopt every unwanted child? Every baby with AIDS? Every desperately disabled child? Are they prepared to fight for housing, health care, education—just plain *food*? Will they cherish and love every battered child?

And when will I hear more pro-choice women speak of the constitutional rights of every American baby to be wanted, loved, and nurtured? Too few people are talking about the children who are tearing this country apart because of their unbearable suffering. And for me, having spent all my younger years in love with childhood, this is the most bitter pill of old age.

Both groups ought to stop marching and screaming, and together they could raise millions of dollars for birth-control counseling centers in every neighborhood in every city. And maybe focus all that energy on directing legislators to show more concern about the quality of life for all living children.

Leaping Into the Past

FOR ANYONE WHO TAKES PRIDE IN KEEPING UP WITH modern trends—pretending to understand the words of rock-and-roll, struggling to sit on cushions on the floor, own home computers and microwaves—more power to you. Whatever turns you on. For me, I am trying in every way I can to leap into the past; the only things I want to take with me are antibiotics and modern surgical skills.

This morning when I woke up, a cardinal was drinking at the fountain in front of my office window. A little while later two ducks appeared, waiting for a breakfast of cracked corn. Yesterday I took my husband's raincoat to the tailor's to see if there was any hope of resuscitation; the store owner and I talked for fifteen minutes about men and clothes, and she told me where we could buy a new coat (for a big, tall man) that wouldn't break us financially.

I went into the bank to deposit a check; no line, immediate service, a pleasant talk about the weather with the cashier. I also had to stop at a hardware store, where the salesperson greeted me by name (I have lived in his town for only five-and-a-half months). When I went to swim, the lifeguard asked me a lot of questions about what courses in psychology she should take to become a nursery-school teacher.

Today I bought several flowering plants, but the salesman told me it was much too early to buy tomato plants and he simply would not sell them to me. Too much pride in his field of expertise.

It has occurred to me that life was much easier, more informal and friendly, a century or so ago. True, I couldn't buy frozen foods no matter how friendly the storekeepers, and indoor plumbing was primitive at best, and wooden wheels and cobblestone streets would have long since broken my back. No matter what the movies may suggest about going backward, it can't be done, and I guess I wouldn't want to because my husband might well have died from his heart attack without current treatments and medication. I don't glorify the present or the past, but I have to confess that there are certain things that were lovely that we could still bring back if we wanted to: for example, friendship and trust between neighbors—not necessarily over a backyard fence, but sitting down with a group and finding ways to help each other. Or making time in our lives to enjoy nature's remaining wonders and pleasures—the funny way a duck waddles, the nest a robin is building using hair discarded outside when I gave my husband a trim, rejoicing in a hyacinth I didn't remember planting, listening to the sound of waves lapping at the shore of a lake.

In some ways everything has changed; in some ways

change has been exhausting, frustrating, cruel; in some ways change can be modified to "fit" us better.

"Old-fashioned" is not a dirty word. Now that I live in the country, I never see a building over two stories high. It is aesthetically pleasing to the eye and calming to the spirit. It reminds me of a study done by the Department of Mental Health of New York State many years ago in which there was unanimous agreement that a cottage-type architecture helped people recover. So new skyscrapers were built! We need to pay more attention to human needs now or we will all have to leap into the past.

III

LIFE STYLES

Living Arrangements

A WOMAN, WHO IS NOW FORTY-THREE YEARS OLD, wrote me, "My mother is seventy-two years old, and she still carries on all the time because I'm not married and having children. She acts as if she is in a constant state of mourning. I have two brothers who are married, and she has three grandchildren already. How can I stop this nagging, this infernal suffering?"

This woman continued: "I have a wonderful job, I have lots of friends, my apartment is perfect for me; I have a boyfriend and we see each other just often enough to suit us both. We like a lot of privacy and freedom. I feel I am living a life that is just right for me."

I guess all I can suggest is that she reassure her mother, tell her exactly how she feels, and agree that this lifestyle is not better than any other but, for example, certainly no worse than married people who have children and then divorce. If Mom needs to suffer, the most important thing is not to get unhinged about it, not to argue about it, and not to feel guilty for not measuring up to someone else's dream.

Since I have often written about marriage, because that has been my personal experience, I still have great respect for people who have chosen another life style because they understand their own needs and respect themselves enough to fulfill themselves in their own way. Misunderstandings about life styles still crop up all the time.

For example, my husband and I were having a special birthday party for a friend. All the guests were close friends, and most of us had attended college together. One man, whom we love a lot, a sweet, gentle, talented man, came alone; his partner of thirty-eight years would not come with him. "I tried hard to assure my partner how special you all are but he is afraid of meeting new people." What his partner was worrying about, we knew, was that he had never recovered from the frequent occasions when he had been rebuffed because he was a homosexual. It made us sad, we felt deprived of his company among the rest of us old married folk. We knew this was one of the most happy and meaningful partnerships—these mature, responsible partners are able to give each other a sustained and loving relationship, and both are successful in their own fields and have close ties to their families. They seem to me to have all the attributes I require for being loved and respected.

A woman, who is seventy-eight, wrote saying she felt it was time to sell her house and move to a retirement community: "After forty years of running a big house, I want a cozy little nest among people my own age. My grown, married children are furious. They can't believe I could leave the home where they were all raised. They were, of course, terribly upset when their father died, and now they want me to guard their memories by not moving. It's just too heavy a burden."

Everyone needs to feel the right to have living arrangements that best express one's personality and changing needs. The struggle to find one's natural living arrangements is a clear expression of concern for what is best in each of us. Nobody should stop us from this worthy pursuit.

Goodbye to Ties and Girdles

MY HUSBAND AND I WENT TO THE AIRPORT TO meet a friend we hadn't seen for about ten years. She looked at us and laughed and said, "You two look like a seedy old flower child and a bag lady!" We couldn't have been more pleased. Our approach to old age was paying off.

When my husband, Larry, was a young man he wore rimless glasses, a white shirt and tie, and had shiny hair well saturated with some greasy stuff. He carefully repressed a lot of feelings he thought were dangerous. He was a proper fellow, concerned with what others thought of him, and endured the strangulation of ties about ninety percent of the time without even complaining.

At the age of twelve my mother decided it was time for me to wear a girdle. I perceived this item of torture as a valid necessity for the next forty or fifty years. When, for example, I traveled with a little baby, I wore a hat, high heels, stockings, and that inevitable harness of a girdle. It wasn't easy with a baby who might throw up and eliminate all waste products into a diaper. There were leaky bottles, messy jars of baby food, and lots of howling to contend with on a number of airlines that were never overjoyed to see us coming. But I put on a brave front and wondered if I would be a disgrace to the civilized world if I took off my three-inch high heels. I didn't do this often—my feet usually swelled and then I would have to endure the pain of forcing my shoes back on.

The flower children of the sixties, bless them, began to make an impression on us. Now Larry has one tie he saves for weddings and funerals. I haven't worn a girdle—even on television!—for seven or eight years. And the world has not yet ended. The signs that the planet may very well blow up have nothing to do with what we are wearing.

I now conclude that one of the greatest joys of old age is "getting loose." We haven't lost a single valued friend. Travel has become a romp. At times my daughter does seem somewhat ashamed of us, but that's been true since she was eleven and made us stand behind a pillar in the school gym when we were chaperoning a sixth-grade dance.

Don't get me wrong; we may never look good enough to be photographed by *Vogue* but we are clean and smell okay. Larry lives in jeans, and very loose slacks and loose dresses are perfect for me. I cut his hair and sometimes think he's a slob, but still find him very handsome. He, poor demented man, calls me names that embarrass but delight me. We are capable of going to weddings and funerals and lectures and dinners, and while "sartorial splendor" is not an expression that comes to anyone's mind, we are presentable. Handsome and gorgeous are not words that ever occur to us; we wear our thinning hair and wrinkles and hanging flesh with ease because old age, we feel, permits us to be the truest selves we have ever been. While I don't believe we frighten people or even disgust them, comfort and freedom are the essence of our lives. Sloppy we may often be, but what energy we now have is more than likely to be going into our work, which continues to thrive in spite of a few major setbacks from accidents and illness. However, we do anticipate a time when our granddaughter might ask us to hide behind a pillar. We wish to avoid that, so we keep our dressy clothes in shape for an emergency. One thing is for sure; she will never wear a girdle if I have any say in the matter.

An Interesting Test

A WOMAN, RECENTLY WIDOWED, WROTE ME: "I
have been feeling very old—glad not to be working at
a job that had become boring, anxious about how to
spend the rest of my life. I have always been sorry I
didn't get a better education so I could have become a
college history teacher. After reading something you
wrote, 'It is never too late to find a dream,' I went out
and got the catalogue of a nearby college. As part of
being admitted, I had to write a composition. I decided
to write two obituaries! If I died right now all that could
have been said was that I was widowed and retired. If
I went back to school, what else might my obituary say,
in some distant future?"

On the second page of the letter was a hand-made
New York Times obituary, dated well into the twenty-
first century, with a picture. There was a long article
describing the excellent work of a history professor who
had written several very valuable books about the
changes in the British monarchy and the reign of Prince
Charles as king. "She will be deeply mourned by the
students and faculty of Princeton University, her children, and grandchildren."

What an absolutely splendid (even if slightly morbid) way to get in touch with one's dreams! A good exercise for anyone feeling depressed or weighed down by self-pity, or feeling paralyzed to move on with one's life. What would your first "obituary" be like? Would you be proud to have been that person, or does it give a message of frustration, disappointment, an unfulfilled life?

At a time when my husband was working as a psychotherapist, one of his patients was in despair. She said, "It's too late, too late. I'm too old to change my life." She had wanted to spend the rest of her life teaching disabled children but she didn't have the educational training she needed. She had been a successful business woman but felt her life had been a meaningless pursuit of money and power. My husband said, "If you wanted to start over, what would be the first thing you would have to do?" The patient had no idea—she mentioned moving, getting a divorce, deserting her teen-age child. My husband kept probing for the "first thing" and finally told her, "The first thing is to get a college catalogue." Very often the initial step, the simplest part of a plan, can lead to a whole new life without any major changes. Six years later this woman, feeling wonderful, in the same house with the same husband and a son in graduate school, is a full-time teacher in a school for severely retarded children.

"I came along at the right moment," she says. "Just when we would have so many new kinds of aids for these children. I've never been happier."

One of the happiest experiences was getting an invitation to a college graduation from a woman I didn't know. In the accompanying letter she wrote, "Before reading your book on middle age I had decided my life was over and I might as well be dead. That was four years ago. My life is just beginning."

Thinking about oneself as dead can be the beginning of a new life.

How a Friend Might Change
My Life

A PROFESSIONAL COLLEAGUE OF MINE FOR MANY years has retired, moved some distance from New York, and feels that he will finally have time to become a full-time sculptor—a dream previously denied because of the pressures of earning a living. Even before retirement he had bought a kiln and whenever he had free time he worked at his art, giving his friends presents of small statues, but always saying, "My longing is to work BIG! To have the time and the space to expand."

He is widowed, and his children are grown and on their own. He now lives in a converted barn in the middle of a meadow on an abandoned farm in the South. It happens to be located near a large university to which my husband was recently invited to speak. I wrote to my friend that we might be near his new home, and I wished him lots of luck on his new full-time career. I admit I figured I'd get a letter saying something like, "Terrific! I'd love to see you. Hope you and Larry can come for dinner."

I got a letter all right, and very promptly. What it said

was, "I hope you'll drop in for a minute and say hello." There were two choices open to me: to feel deeply offended and rejected, or to learn a valuable lesson from a perfect role model.

I admit it hurt a little, but he really gave me just the gift I needed the most—a clear picture of what's the matter with me.

It was a message my innermost mind has been trying hard to give me but I haven't paid enough attention. I dream of a little girl who has chicken pox, or is all alone, deserted by others, or is running away but never really gets anywhere, like the White Queen in *Alice in Wonderland*. Finally, my distant friend has made me pay attention; *I* want to tell other people what he told me: "This is my time, don't bother me."

I will never really go as far as he did. Love, compassion, and ethical standards, which have been too high all my life, will keep me from achieving what he has! But I sure better *try*. I feel fractured, frustrated, and angry too often because I don't protect my time and energy. There is less of these qualities every day—time is *not* on my side. Every day there is another shock; I hear about something that happened five or seven years ago, and it seems to me it happened at the most a week ago. The pages on my calendar flip faster every month.

To some degree most of us need to be able to say, "Come say hello for a minute," instead of making a dinner date and cooking the guest's favorite dishes all day. Time is more precious every moment, and it is not selfish to want to fulfill our own dreams before it's too late.

An Unexpected Passion

I HOPE YOU WON'T BE TOO SHOCKED BUT I AM passionately in love, and it's not my husband I'm talking about.

It's Peaches, who happens to be a marmalade kitten— more beautiful than any you may have seen on a box of cat food. I have never been in love with a cat before, and like all affairs of the heart, it is both wonderful and terrible.

I took a major risk last fall and moved to Cape Cod. From November to March, I lived through eight incredible snowstorms. I couldn't have survived without Peaches.

For several years, I have had a picture in my head of the perfect cat, all orange and white with a striped tail. I decided to believe in my husband's California-style philosophy that you just have to trust some mystical pattern and wait. I used to think that was a little to the left of nutty as a fruitcake, but the way this cat arrived has made me a member of the club.

Peaches was one of a litter, born in Vermont and about to be drowned (too many cats on the farm), when a friend of mine who knew of my fantasy saved him. The cat was six weeks old, and we weren't sure of the sex, but my granddaughter came up with the perfect name, non-gender specific, as they say, for this cat was surely the color of peach marmalade.

Being alone together much of the time, Peaches and I have over-bonded. Early in our love affair, I could not bear it when this tiny cat was sick, and when I have to leave for frequent trips to New York, I am inconsolable.

Peaches feels the same way about me. He sits on my typewriter and purrs loudly, making it clear I have to give up writing and pay attention only to him. He follows me to the bathroom and climbs on my lap. He also knocks over the garbage, tries to rip every piece of furniture in the house, and, one day, flew into the refrigerator when I didn't close the door fast enough. He got lost for three hours when I accidentally closed a closet door—I almost went into cardiac arrest before I figured out where he was.

We have compromised on his never letting me out of his sight—he is now sleeping on a chair next to my typewriter, and I wish you could see him. He just looked at me with his great yellow eyes. I think he knows I am writing about him.

I never before had a cat that was all mine. In fact, I merely tolerated my daughter's cats. I wonder if it is age that now makes me feel guilty for all the times I made fun of cat people. Maybe it's being mostly alone-in-the-snow for five months (we'll see, now that spring is here). Maybe it's just a new appreciation of beauty.

I suspect it is primarily old age. I appreciate the important things in life more than I ever did before. Every day Peaches teaches me about unconditional love—that no matter how naughty he is, I will love him, and that no matter how mad I get, he will love me. That makes the love affair of my declining years one of my richer learning experiences.

AT&T Should Give Me a Bonus

MANY YEARS AGO I WROTE AN ARTICLE ENTITLED "The Teen-ager and the Telephone," which appeared in *McCall's Magazine*. I had a teen-age daughter then and was suffering like most other parents about the amount of time our kids spent on the phone in the afternoon and evening with friends they'd seen all day in school. It was annoying and expensive.

Then one day I heard a conversation between my husband and another psychotherapist. They were discussing the fact that certain seriously disturbed patients seemed to make more progress by telephone therapy sessions than in personal contacts. I pricked up my ears when one of them commented, "Face-to-face relationships are too threatening, but the telephone allows for contact in a safer way."

At last! I had found the answer to the telephonitis of adolescents! I realized that these children, so self-conscious, trying so hard to make contact with each other, and feeling so unsure of how to develop necessary social relations, could make easier contact (to talk about personal feelings) if they were not looking at each other.

And what, you may well be asking, has that got to do
with those of us now getting long in the tooth. I have
a friend of whom I am very fond, but she has been
exasperating me beyond endurance because her telephone line is busy sometimes for four and five hours a
day. The other day when I was yelling at her for the
hundredth time, she said, "Eda, I am seventy-eight years
old. Many of my friends—those still alive—can't get out
to meet each other the way we used to. Everybody I
know my age and older has health problems or lives in
unsafe neighborhoods and can't go out at night. We
would lose touch with each other, be completely iso-
lated, if we couldn't talk to each other on the phone."
So here I am, second time around, giving an unsolicited
endorsement for the telephone! My friend was absolutely right and made me do some renewed thinking
about the fact that there are two appropriate times in
the course of our lives when the telephone is a special
asset for maintaining social relationships—when we are
young and shy and when we are old and lonely.

I no longer feel angry or frustrated when anyone my
age or older has a busy line for many hours. I know that
what is happening is that important friendships are being
sustained; that family contacts are not being lost because
of the massive mobility that pulls people from place to
place; that grandchildren can feel the loving watchful-
ness of faraway grandparents; that the widowed, the
single, the chronically ill have a lifeline and can continue
to feel a sense of connection with those whom they care
about. But before you assume I'm looking for a bonus
from AT&T (or at least a kiss from Cliff Robertson!) I

ought to add that I, personally, hate to talk on the telephone and would rather write twenty four-page letters than try to communicate seriously over one phone call. I am a throwback to the letter-writing generations before Alexander Bell. And I have the advantage of being able to read the letters I get more than once, and even save some for the next generation, if they are really special.

But I have a new tolerance for busy lines and suggest that in order to share the pleasure I have in saving letters, those who prefer to use the phone can tape special calls for future listening. Just be sure you tell the other party what you are doing!

When the Best-Laid Plans Run Into Trouble

As I sat at the typewriter one day when I was still living in the city, looking out the window, two pigeons nestled cozily next to a large plastic owl on the small terrace of my office-apartment. Four other pigeons hovered in the air nearby. This was not supposed to happen. Our best-laid plans had run afowl. (Editor: Please don't change to afoul; let me have my little joke.)

It was like this: The terrace was just too small to accommodate people and pigeons, and we had decided in favor of human beings, despite my love of the bird world. Their "gifts" made it impossible for us to inhabit the same area. Country folk and catalogues of companies devoted to the great outdoors all assured us that a fake owl would scare off the pigeons. So we bought one for twelve dolloars. In order to make it stand up straight I lugged a few hundred small stones from a nearby wooded path up to my apartment and put them into the owl through a hole for this purpose on its bottom. I had to be away for a few days and returned to find almost every square foot of the terrace covered in pigeon doo;

the pigeons thought the owl was their mother, obviously, and bonding was in full swing. We removed the
owl, tried spraying the terrace with ammonia and bleach,
but I could see it was going to be a fight to the death.
The pigeons remembered Mama.

This was a great metaphor for life. How often our
well-laid plans run into trouble! We've had tickets to
our favorite opera tucked away for two months and get
the flu the day before; we have planned a trip to a tropical
isle, and two days before our departure, there is a hur-
ricane which has blown down the hotel; we have planned
a wonderful dinner party, having finally found a date
when all our favorite people are available, only to break
a leg going to the cellar to get some jars of divine home-
made pickles. We have promised to take a grandchild
on a picnic and it rains for five days straight.

So far I've described nothing too devastating, all open
to flexibility and creative re-planning. But one can't talk
about best-laid plans to those of us over sixty with
merely a light touch and a bemused heart. I must have
gotten more than one hundred letters in the last few
years conveying a message similar to that of the widow
who wrote: "We had planned this trip to Africa for four
years, waiting for all our kids to grow up and get through
college, so we'd have a little money. My husband had a
heart attack and died the week before we were to leave."
Another person over sixty wrote: "We planned to build
a little cabin on a lake when my father died and left us
enough money to fulfill this dream. Within a few months
of his death my mother developed Alzheimer's and all
the money has to be used for her care."

How do we deal with the trivial disappointments of life as well as the genuine tragedies? Not easily. It helps if we have always acknowledged that such things can happen. It helps if there have always been alternative thoughts in our head. It helps if we are flexible, courageous, and have learned to "throw the owl out"— bringing humor and creativity to the problem, while not afraid to cry and shake our fists at Fate, when that seems appropriate.

Disappointment, even heartache, calls on us to use our natural talents to the fullest degree, and to always be ready to make new plans.

A New Definition of "Family"

ONE HUNDRED OR MORE YEARS AGO THE DEFINI-
tion of a family would have been mothers, fathers, children, grandparents, aunts, and uncles, more often than
not, living together on a farm, in a rural house, in a city
brownstone, or in a tenement. My immigrant father at
the turn of the last century thought nothing of sleeping
in a bed with two brothers, an uncle, and a cousin. My
great aunt Minna, who never married, was an essential
member of her sister's household; she was babysitter,
seamstress, and second-in-command in the kitchen. Re-
marriages occurred frequently, not by divorce but by
the early death of a spouse. The more hands rocking
the cradle the better, so there were families with eight,
ten, or even a dozen children.

Some time ago I saw the Broadway play *Falsettos*.
More than anything else it is about new concepts of
family. It reminded me that what constitutes a family
has changed more rapidly during the twentieth century
than in the last five thousand years or maybe even
longer.

The new definition has to do with any number of

people from two on up who deeply care for each other and take responsibility for each other's survival. As a matter of fact, I guess that the truth is that one person can be a family if there is a support group in the wings: For example, a widowed mother who lives alone but has two children and several grandchildren, four neighbors who love her and watch out for her, three cousins from the West Coast who come east once a year to see her, and a minister who comes for tea once a week can constitute a family.

In *Falsettos* there are people who represent the older concept of family—parents, a child, marriage. But with a difference. The parents are divorced, and the marriage is between two homosexuals. Other members of the family are not blood relatives, but friends who fulfill the universal timeless functions of family members—sharing grief and joy, taking care of each other, struggling to understand, forgive, and strengthen ties that bind them together. It is a deeply moving testament to the simple fact that a family is a place where people love each other.

It is not easy for those of us who are more used to the traditional view of family life to adapt to single-parent families, to a lesbian couple with two adopted children, to an apartment arrangement where two un-married women with children share life, expenses, feelings, and responsibilities with an interracial married couple and three young adults recovering from drug abuse. Not exactly the picture created by *Life with Father* by Clarence Day, not exactly *Leave It to Beaver*.

One of the first—and wonderful—examples of the

new concept of family life was in *The Mary Tyler Moore* series, showing several families converging in a house with multiple apartments as well as depicting the more extended family of the staff of a TV news program. Families choose each other now. Or sometimes external forces create families. When one watches visitors to the Vietnam Memorial wall hugging, kissing, and holding on to each other for dear life, one senses that a healing process is taking place among strangers who have become family.

Our children and grandchildren want us to be part of their lives. But they want us to greet new kinds of family members. Since the family remains the most civilizing force in the world, we had better adjust.

IV

'TIL DEATH DO US PART (AND OTHER ARRANGEMENTS)

Letting Go in Order to Stay Close

SPRING HAS SPRUNG ON CAPE COD, WHERE I WANT to spend the rest of my life (I think, right now—who knows?). I can have my breakfast outdoors, looking at flowering trees, birds, the nearby woods turning a fuzzy green. It is all so perfect, so beautiful it takes my breath away. But my husband, Larry, wakes up feeling restless and depressed; he came to stay with me in the country for ten days, but when I say how happy I am, I suddenly realize that all this natural beauty, quiet, and peace is driving him nuts. He is longing for his dark New York office, facing brick walls; he is missing the honking horns, the sirens, the dirty streets, the tall buildings that shut out the sky and the sun. He is homesick for a place where I know I could never live again.

What shall I do? I tell him what I see in his face, and he agrees. He looks happier already. What pleases me is that I don't feel rejected or unloved. We have both learned we have to accept each other's needs or give up living fully. I must say he is far more understanding of my need to live in nature than I am about his chosen surroundings. I tell him that hopefully there will soon be better connections between Hyannis and New York, and with special senior citizen rates we might be able to afford flying back and forth more easily. He could come here for three days instead of ten. My feelings are mixed. I will be lonely some of the time when he leaves, but there is also a feeling I might get to work and do some writing I've been wanting to do. Having now been honest with each other, I know we will have much more fun for the time we are together.

I know our circumstances are unusual and surely not everybody's lifestyle. I know it would not be realistic for most people and is only possible for us because we are both still working. But I think there is a general message in what we are doing for others with perhaps more limited possibilities. It is critical, for example, to recognize that each person in a marriage has different needs and ways of growing, and neither partner should feel rejected if one wants to take a course in the history of geological formations in the Rockies and the other can't think of anything more boring and wants to go to the theater with some friends every month or so. It is important not to feel angry and forlorn when one feels like spending a day in a library and the other wants to go to a tennis match. It means not going shopping together unless you both love it; it means seeing friends you don't both like, separately. What it boils down to is separate lives are essential for being close. Anger festers if either partner feels so totally needed by the other that there is no room to breathe.

Of course I win on that subject; I breathe in the scent of flowers, grass, and trees, while Larry breathes garbage, carbon monoxide, smoke, and dog doo.

Each to his own.

When Your Spouse Drives You Crazy

During one of our infrequent, but intense shouting matches, my husband uttered, "You write all these books about people driving each other crazy—you should write one for us!"

What a good idea! First I wrote a book called *When Your Child Drives You Crazy*. An eight-year-old boy was very angry about that title, so I explained to him that the reason children drive adults crazy is because the grownups don't understand the children. He accepted that, and then he said, "You should write a book for kids about parents driving *them* crazy," so I did. After that book was published, I was invited to speak at an elementary school, and later one of the children there wrote me a letter saying, "I wish you'd write a book about how kids drive kids crazy," so I did. This crazy theme always came down to people of any age going nuts when they didn't understand the people they were dealing with. Why hadn't I realized before that husbands and wives are a prime example of this dilemma?

My main theses in each of the earlier books was that people don't understand each other because they can't remember their own childhood. When we can remember the past, we learn to live with present problems. Sometimes, for example, my husband drives me crazy because he could spend the rest of his life in a university library. What I have learned about him is that in the midst of what the younger generation calls a "dysfunctional family" he escaped from his miseries through reading and through private intellectual pursuits. What has often driven him crazy about me is that I can yell a lot about dirty clothes not being put in the hamper, dirty dishes in the sink for two days, or piles of twenty or thirty old newspapers on the dining-room table. He knows that my mother used to tear my room apart on a Saturday morning and make me spend the day cleaning it up.

If we begin to take a second look at the things that bother us the most about a spouse, we should be able to get a better perspective and manage some necessary compromises. This can be applied to sexual hang-ups, temper tantrums, absent-mindedness, waves of irrational jealousy, and lack of trust. Surely some of the things that drive us crazy are differences in temperament, but the past also plays a major role. I know one man who wants an accounting of every penny his wife spends; he never had an allowance. I know another man who cannot do anything his wife asks him to do around the house. He had an abusive mother and ran away from home at seventeen. Deep inside he harbors a feeling that he can't let a woman control him in any way. A woman friend feels terribly threatened and uncomfortable about being naked in front of her husband. As a fat child she was constantly being ridiculed. Although her husband thinks she's beautiful she can't let go of her earlier shame. An adult who always felt less loved than a sibling is likely to be jealous; if parents lie to a child, he or she may never quite trust a spouse.

The best solution when marriage partners drive each other crazy is getting some professional help to gain insight into each other's foibles and hopefully open up some room for allowance. It doesn't work one hundred percent of the time but it helps. For instance, I like to arrive at the airport two hours early, but Larry gets there with ten minutes to spare. Whatever the childhood causes may be, we compromise and get to airports forty-five minutes early. After years of exploring past causes of our unique neuroses, it becomes possible to take some shortcuts.

How to Be Incompatible for Forty-Nine Years

IT WAS PROBABLY A MISTAKE, BUT A FEW YEARS AGO my husband and I had an idea for a sort of a funny little book that was supposed to help couples decide if they were compatible or not. The idea was to save them from making a bad mistake in choosing the wrong person for a commitment. When we began listing possible items, it was clear that we had made a serious mistake in marrying each other forty-nine years ago.

I like a window open at night and the steam heat turned off; he likes to close the windows and he loves radiators that give me a headache when going full blast. I turn off the light even if I am only leaving a room for five minutes. He doesn't turn off the lights even if he's going out for the whole day. He has every book, letter, and journal that ever came his way. I throw at least five things out every day.

He wouldn't care if he never bought a new piece of clothing or had his hair cut again. He owns one tie, for funerals only. I'm very conscious of at least being reasonably neat in public. It makes me nervous when he has to give an important speech to some really august group, in his turtleneck, in a room of 1499 men with ties on.

Larry would be happy to spend every waking moment in the library. He reads *The Encyclopedia Britannica* for pleasure. He is so learned he can recite several hundred poems by heart and knows every writer, soldier, and politician who lived in Greece in 450 B.C., and at the same time he likes to watch every James Bond movie, *Star Wars*, and *Star Trek* as often as humanly possible. I can't quote a single poem, hate looking anything up, even in the telephone book, and want my books and movies to be romantic, on the order of *It Happened One Night* and *Moonstruck*.

I am an early riser, often at my typewriter by 5 A.M. He's a night person, often burns the midnight oil, and likes to sleep late. I want to make the bed every day; he'd never make it if left to his own inclinations. I like seeing friends once in a while; he always growls at any dinner dates. The list goes on and on, but the problem is we can't imagine being married to anyone else. It might seem to be incomprehensible that we're still together, but it's not because of the things we agree about. Each of us thinks the other one is adorable, exciting, talented. We both miss Eleanor Roosevelt. We worked side by side for better race relations when we lived in the South during World War II. We always vote for anyone who we think will help the most disenfranchised, poorest, least educated, often homeless people. We agree on all major social issues.

We love Paris and London. Each of us finds the other

the most interesting person we know. Commitment is not about who puts the top on the toothpaste and squeezes from the bottom (that's me). What commitment requires is a passionate love of each other and a capacity to go on growing. It also means being open to adventure and having a special tenderness for all living things, including our weary, war-torn planet. And most of all, it demands an absolute belief in the right—the need—of allowing one's partner the fullest expression of being him- or herself. Of course, there are those moments when he forgets to give me telephone messages and I remind him twenty times to take something to the cleaners—but the trivialities of life have nothing to do with total commitment to each other.

Finances in Later Loves and Lives

IN FORTY-NINE YEARS OF MARRIAGE NOT ONCE HAVE my husband and I ever spoken of "his money" and "my money." It has seemed to us that love, trust, and teamwork influence every aspect of a relationship, including the full sharing of financial resources. But I can see that even if a couple has had that philosophy in a first marriage, everything seems to be quite different in a second marriage, or when living together, or just being in love and not living together.

I know this from the many letters I receive. A sixty-eight-year-old widow wrote that she's contemplating a second marriage but is worried about keeping her own money intact when she dies so it will be inherited by her children. A man of seventy-four writes, "Isn't it selfish if the woman I'm now living with wants me to pay for everything?" And in another letter a retired sixty-four-year-old man living on a small fixed income writes that he is planning to marry a woman who has inherited a fortune and he doesn't want to ever be beholden to her. He is annoyed that she wants to take trips and live in a lifestyle he can't afford. "She will destroy my manhood," he wrote, "unless I pay my own way."

Balderdash, I say! I find it strange and alien to see how money can become a symbol for personal feelings or attitudes about oneself. Money seems to become a metaphor through which people play out their self-doubts, their feelings of unworthiness, their distrust of life itself.

If I were a widow (I can barely even write the words) and I fell in love with a wealthy man, I would not have the slightest qualms about joining his lifestyle! I would hope we would both have much more fun than either of us could have alone. If I had the money, I'd happily share it. But men of our generation were taught that a "real man" could never be "kept" by a woman.

I would surely advise any older couple to see a tax-and-will expert about resources each wants to leave to children or charitable organizations. Beyond that, financial assets for daily living ought to be shared in love and joy—or, if they can't be, it seems to me it is time to re-evaluate not only the relationship but what each partner is bringing to it in terms of feelings of worthiness or self-doubts. Love to me means sharing, commitment, and not withholding; it means the most profound kind of mutual trust and the fervent wish to use all resources available for getting the most out of life while it lasts. If one or both partners are fearful, suspicious, or secretive, then according to my standards, that ain't love.

Love, companionship, and friendship later in life is so precious it ought not be squandered by "his" or "hers" before death. Afterwards when kids and creditors line up for the goodies, the romance will have remained intact. I am absolutely convinced that if Romeo and Juliet had met when they were over sixty-five and each alone, whose money they lived on would have been the last thing on their minds.

Are Husbands or Wives More Accommodating?

I AM THOROUGHLY ASHAMED OF MYSELF: WHEN two couples, neighbors, were arguing about whether men or women (middle-aged and older) were more likely to "give in," upon being asked for my opinion, I had a moment of self-pity and impulsively replied too spontaneously, "Oh, women are much more accommodating." The two women were delighted with my response, and the whole thing bothered me all day long.

It is true that I accept certain realities that I could happily live without: leaving the toilet seat up, letting the hamper overflow but never considering doing the laundry, ten thousand books piled on every available shelf and floor space, always bringing home the wrong items from the supermarket, going to sleep after a fight, refusing to go to family gatherings if humanly possible . . . oh, I could run amok with it all.

But then, unfortunately, sanity and fairness hit. He accommodated me about toilet etiquette; he goes with me when the dentist is going to do something awful; he took care of me after two major operations and a stroke. He has endured my extravagant mood swings for forty-nine years although they drive him crazy. He has tolerated my tendency towards pessimism and my view that the weather is deliberately and personally against me.

At a time we surely couldn't afford it, he told me to take a year off from work and try to become a writer. He used to go to see plays that didn't really interest him—until I learned to go alone and like it.

I accommodated myself to working at several jobs when he had a research grant that couldn't possibly cover our expenses—and years later, when his research became known here and abroad and saved lives, I felt it was my victory as well as his.

The truth of the matter is that in a good and long-lasting marriage, men and women are constantly accommodating each other. Women are inclined to get annoyed about the domestic inconveniences and men are more likely to be annoyed by women's tendencies towards emotional irrationality, but what makes the whole thing work is the areas in which we share the give-and-take of life most dramatically. We take care of each other when we are sick; we grieve together for the loss of a loved one; we shared all the crises of child-raising. Together we went through the miseries and joys of getting along with relatives, bosses, and co-workers.

I get chills when I hear him introduced at a conference as someone who has inspired colleagues; he cries at the plays I write, even if no one else thinks they are any good. Give-and-take is the name of the game, and I must see to it immediately that these two couples who were arguing about men and women accommodating each other get a copy of this final report.

I'll Take the Flowers

TRY TO GET THIS PICTURE: SOMEHOW I HAVE managed to lower my stiff and overweight body to the hall floor in my apartment. I had bought a piece of carpeting to be used as a hall runner, to cover worn spots in the main carpeting, which would have cost thousands of dollars to replace. My husband had promised me this morning that he'd come home early to help me with binding and hammering in the carpet tacks, because I have arthritis in both knees and getting up and down is now painful, if not entirely impossible. But what I have discovered, now that I am on the floor, is that I can't get up. I started this project two hours after the expected arrival of my helpmate, and now I am fuming. I am in a rage. I mutter about his selfishness and his thoughtlessness, and I feel terribly sorry for myself. I realize that I am going to have to sit on the floor until he comes home to help me get up. I've only done half the job and my back is killing me. When That Man walks in the door, boy, is he going to *get it*.

The door opens. I see at once that he is carrying a bunch of my favorite flowers. He is contrite; he says he was sure I wouldn't start without him. Now I am twice as angry because I can't yell at him.

Happily married couples will recognize this as a normal afternoon. Widowed men and women, I'm sure, are thinking, "That ungrateful wretch—she still has her spouse—she should appreciate her good fortune."

Absolutely true. I laugh. I acknowledge how mad I was getting. Together we manage to get me to a standing position—and I thank him for the flowers. I know how lucky I am—and I almost never forget the anguish of some of my lonely friends.

But for those of us who are still married to our best friend, who have weathered some of the awful crises and hazards of a long life together and wouldn't go through some of it again for love or money, but think a good deal about what it will be like when one of us dies and the other is left alone, I think it's important not to avoid confrontations just because this fear becomes more and more real as we get older and witness so many new widowhoods.

It is impossible to live in a close relationship without frustration, without losing patience, without someone being thoughtless—without conflict. The problem is that we are human. It is pointless to try to avoid confrontations. If we deny our anger or hurt feelings, if we try to hold our tempers, we will destroy the very thing we want so much to hold on to—a living, breathing, genuine relationship of intense communication and love.

I took my flowers and was grateful he was home safely, and we went on from that crisis, knowing there would be others, but never forgetting to affirm the love. We take the bad moments, we cherish the good ones, and whatever happens in the future there will be no regrets about anger and misunderstanding. It is part of the package. It is part of being fully alive.

Passion Knows No Age

My FRIEND SYLVIA IS SEVENTY-SEVEN YEARS OLD. At the moment she looks about fourteen, she blushes easily, sighs, flashes her eyes, blinks her eyelashes provocatively, is so adolescent that I found myself looking for acne! She was horrified on a recent trip to New York that she had forgotten to bring a picture of her eighty-five-year-old lover. From her description, I figure he looks like a slightly older combination of Tyrone Power, Gregory Peck, and Clark Gable. He is also the most talented artist who ever lived (my impression is that this includes Picasso, Monet, and Van Gogh).

We met for lunch, and Sylvia said, "I suppose you think this is pretty obscene," after she had made it quite clear this was a total passion, which means physical as well as spiritual. *She* didn't mean it for a minute—I guess she was testing my reaction, which was, "How perfectly divine!" My husband's reaction was, "Go, girl, go!" I think we passed the test.

This visit reminded me of something younger people find it very hard to imagine—that we can still feel passionate about love, at any age, if the circumstances are

right. Previous generations of older people would have
gone into cardiac arrest if anyone had suggested such a
thing; and most of us were probably brainwashed when
we were younger to think we would become asexual
zombies certainly after sixty-five, and more likely after
fifty.

Of course, Sylvia, a widow for several years, never
expected to fall madly in love again. It comes as a surprise to the married as well as the widowed that romance
can still be part of our lives. It may take different forms.
I remember my father once writing me a letter in which
he said, "Passion changes from a wild fire to a quiet
glow." I was sure he was wrong then, but now I think
that can be a very nice state of affairs for some people, though surely not all. I also believe that if passion
disappears, one can still have a rich life of affection
and caring; someone I know quite intimately (initials
L. L.) said, "I'm hungry for a hug." I think that's very romantic.

The point is, whatever form it takes, the attraction
between the sexes surely doesn't disappear with hot
flashes or arthritic knees. Sometimes there can be a
startling new love with all the old passions. Sometimes
it may be simply reawakening our sense of excitement
because of a special holiday, or the suddenly sharpened
awareness of love when a partner is ill, or sharing the
first look at the first grandchild.

What does it every time for me is that my husband is
very tall and if we plan to meet at a movie theater or a
restaurant on a crowded street, I can see him very
quickly. After forty-nine years I feel my heart quicken,

I feel a passionate excitement—here comes the most important person in my life. Sylvia's new love is wonderful, but I am very content with not having to be fourteen again. It was exciting, but being seventy-two and in love with the old familiar guy suits me fine.

Bedroom Strategies

Sorry, folks, this isn't about sex; well, maybe it is in a roundabout way.

When I was young and newly married, we visited the home of *some truly elderly people* in their sixties. Their age was bad enough, but my conviction that they were on their last legs was confirmed by the fact that *they had separate bedrooms!* I was appalled; did romance end when a couple got *that* old? What a terrible thing to anticipate.

Well, it is a shameful confession but, at seventy-four and seventy-two respectively, my husband and I have our problems sharing a bedroom; an even worse confession—when we sleep in our separate office/homes there is sometimes a sense of relief. This is not clear and simple—there is, of course, a sense of loss and loneliness, and I have an adorable cat which helps a little— but the real problems start when we share a bedroom.

When Larry goes to bed, he is asleep in about twelve seconds. When I go to bed, I need to read for a while or listen to the radio. He likes the steam heat on and would prefer a temperature more suited to an August day, any time of the year. I choke and cough and get a sore throat from steam heat. Even at his advanced age, he sleeps through the night and I have to get up two or three times for reasons I do not have to explain to this audience. If I wake up during the night, I like to read some more; if he wakes up at night (rarely) he goes inside to watch television, and sooner or later, mostly much later, I can't sleep for worrying how he will get through the next day. Most of the time I get up early. I can't stand the dirty dishes in the sink from the night before and it wakes him up when I wash them.

We would both love to cuddle some of the time when we go to sleep, but my arthritic spine means I can't lie on my side—either way. So we hold hands if Larry doesn't fall asleep before his head hits the pillow, or if I fall asleep first, watching television.

It isn't easy. But there are certain adjustments one can make. A night light in the hall helps any wanderings. A radio with an earphone is essential. Since the bathroom is past the bed, I have to make sure the comforter isn't on the floor impeding my half-blind trips. I buy sleep masks for him as quickly as possible, but he loses them even faster. Now he sleeps with a pillow over his face and I worry he is going to asphyxiate himself.

How often I think of that couple with the two bedrooms. Now they seem to have been incredibly young, and I feel sorry they had to take such drastic steps so early. I hope they crossed the hall some of the time. As for us, romance is alive and well wherever we spend our nights, together or apart. We may have accommodated to certain realities of advancing age, but my arthritis does not interfere with hugs in a standing position.

A Cruise Is Not a Cure for Problems

For our forty-seventh anniversary my husband and I took a cruise to Alaska. The scenery was wonderful, we only yelled at each other once or twice, and in the middle of the summer (having endured the heat of New York) I didn't perspire once in twenty-five days, which was almost worth the whole trip!

I was reminded by listening to some of the conversations on board the ship how wonderful a trip can be for couples who love each other most of the time and how awful traveling can be if we save up some of our most pressing problems and think we can avoid dangerous topics until we get home. I heard one man say to another, "My wife and I have been planning this trip for twenty years and now she announces she doesn't like me!" A subject that surely should have been discussed long before a cruise! Another man commented to the woman sitting next to him at the table that his wife was buying everything in sight. "Why don't you say, 'No'?" the woman asked, and in a whisper he answered, "She'd make me pay in worse ways."

What we sometimes forget is that on a vacation, there is more time for a hidden agenda to emerge. The most unhappy trip I ever took to places I loved was at a time when our marriage was about to blow up. I was in total denial when we started and devastated by its end; it was not a time for us to be traveling, presumably for pleasure. We had a lot of work to do on our marriage.

A very wise therapist, Florence Miale, who helped me greatly and died too soon, assured me that nothing could make marital discord worse than a trip! A vacation can quickly evoke both mental and physical stress that have been buried too long—witness the number of heart attacks that occur sitting at the side of a pool at a hotel.

We should never assume that a vacation trip will wash away tension and unhappiness. If we know we have serious problems that must be faced sooner or later, it is the best part of wisdom to deal with these sooner.

Some married couples neutralize the tensions by traveling with one or more other couples or sitting at tables of eight aboard ship. The maître d' on the *QE II* almost had a nervous breakdown when we insisted on a table for two. He couldn't believe that this was our honest preference. (It isn't that we are horribly anti-social but we have so little time together while working and have to talk to so many people that we need Time Out, especially when we don't say a word to each other, just hold hands and look at the scenery!)

Some friends of ours took a car trip with another couple. They thought the other couple were devoted and happy. It turned out that the trip was a nightmare. Not having faced their marital disaster at home, this couple spent the whole trip fighting about motels, places to eat, directions, whatever details and crises that came up or that they could invent. "We wish they had agreed to a divorce before the trip and saved us a miserable time," our friends told us.

Problems are surely not always that dramatic—maybe a strong disagreement about whether to give a grandchild money for college, or annoyance if one partner wants to retire and the other doesn't. Take my word for it: Tension means taking too much extra baggage.

V

CHILDREN AND GRANDCHILDREN

Enjoying Our Children's Inheritance Now

My daughter and granddaughter own a horse named Bolt. We bought him. Did we discover a gold mine? Did we hit the right stocks or bonds? Are we rich?

None of the above. In fact, our money manager scolded us severely for buying such an extravagant gift. She warned us about a terrible, poverty-stricken old age. She talked to us about future taxes. She assured us we were out of our minds since we had a mortgage on a house in Cape Cod, an apartment in Manhattan, and an unsold apartment in Riverdale. She dared to call us "naughty children." (She's about thirty years younger than we are.) She even suggested it was a federal crime to use our old-age savings on a horse.

But what our money manager wasn't taking into account is something that we have only recently learned ourselves—something we never understood when our daughter, Wendy, was a child. Apparently horses were at the very core of her being. When she went off to camp, it was very clear she rode as if born to the saddle, but we never understood the depth of her love for horses. It was foreign to us.

When our granddaughter began riding, we were afraid it was her mother's earlier longing being expressed, but we were wrong. We began to realize that these two shared a joy beyond measure. The only thing they really wanted in all the world was a horse.

The horse of their dreams materialized: a horse coveted by many others who know about horses and a bargain at twice the price. This was obviously a horse destined to be loved passionately by our child and grandchild. We watched a level of ecstatic happiness that will warm our hearts for the rest of our lives. We've never felt more loved—or as pleased with anything we've given.

We know many people who save every penny they can so they can leave a pile of money to their children and grandchildren when they die. That seems like utter foolishness to us. They will never see the kind of joy we have witnessed. They will never share in the pleasures their money can bring right now. What an awful deprivation!

I don't think we will be homeless or lacking in care when we are in our eighties or nineties. We aren't crazy, I hope. But even if we end up on Medicaid in a nursing home, we will have better memories than those who count their dividends until the end.

This manager of ours told my husband that it was time we started to save for a rainy day. Larry replied, "I've had a heart attack and Eda's had a stroke; it's already pouring outside!"

What Our Grandchildren Missed

MY FRIEND ANNE TOLD ME ABOUT SOMETHING that happened recently with her four-year-old grand-daughter Molly, who asked her, "Grandma, why do you have those funny spots on your hands?" Grandma replied, "That's something that happens when you get old." Molly looked wistful and replied, "Why didn't I know you when you were new?"

That story hit me like a ton of bricks. As I have gotten older myself I have felt more and more regret over the fact that I never saw any of my grandparents when they were young. In spite of photographs I had great trouble imagining them as young men and women.

I now live near my twelve-year-old granddaughter. My hair is getting so thin I think of myself as a molting bird; the big wrinkles have little wrinkles of their own; I move about as swiftly as a World War II army tank. I can't chew steak or eat corn without my upper teeth falling out. What must she really think about this decrepit creature who is me? I was never—oh, my no!— eligible for Miss America, but I was *young*, and that was enough for me to like the face in the mirror. I wish my grandchild could have seen me at sixteen or twenty-five—or even at forty. Vanity about my appearance is something new and quite intolerable; it is something I never cared about before.

I remember very clearly where and when I had my first intimation of what was coming. I was shoveling snow out of my driveway, having moved into a house in New Jersey several days before; I didn't know any of my new neighbors. Suddenly a tall, young woman came leaping over the snow drifts, shouting, "You mustn't do that!" She explained that it was dangerous for "old people" to shovel snow. This happened about fifteen years ago. I was shocked, but I thanked her profusely, assured her I was all right and glad to know I had such a thoughtful neighbor.

But when I got back into the house I headed for the well-lighted bathroom mirror. Good God! I was getting wrinkles! What a shock! Nobody had told me. I got over thinking about it at all until I realized that I wished my granddaughter had seen me before the inevitable decaying process had begun. Maybe when she's older she will be interested in my family albums; she couldn't care less now. She asks my advice about a few things now and that should surely please me enough.

Someone may ask if I've changed my mind about facelifts. No, I don't consider that an alternative. For the same sort of reason why nothing could ever have convinced me to try heroin or cocaine—I valued my mind too much to fool around with it. Unnecessary surgery would be gambling with my life and health, and I sure don't want to fool around with that. Anyway,

I'm such a coward that I've never even had my ears pierced!

There was that momentary, intense pang when I heard about Molly's question, but I tell myself that if I try hard enough my granddaughter may think of me as having a young heart and mind. I will settle for that.

Grandma's Love Letters

TWELVE-YEAR-OLD GIRLS ARE GETTING PREGNANT; fourteen-year-old boys are dying of AIDS. Public officials struggle desperately to give specific advice to school-age children on the unbelievable hazards they face, while others scream about "sin" and would apparently rather see children destroyed than informed. I tried very hard, when the world seemed to be changing too fast for me, to adjust, change my ideas, and be flexible. I did a pretty good job of learning to live with—even sometimes approve of—committed relationships outside of marriage. I even saw some value in movies that had a sharper honesty than the romantic fairy tales of my youth. But now, with a society that allows children to destroy themselves through behavior for which they are too young and to expose themselves to dangers never dreamed of before, I am changing my mind. Let me say it straight out: I wish that no children were allowed to date until sixteen, that all dates were chaperoned, that young people lived at home until they married, and that strict rules of discipline existed in safe homes with parents in charge! There, I said it!

I guess that's "old" again. In the face of irreconcilable problems, I want to go back to a simpler, more constricted society.

I felt completely helpless and in despair, but that all changed when Susan and her granddaughter, Betty, came to see me. Betty, at eighteen, is absolutely beautiful; her smile is radiant. She's loving every minute of college and has terrific goals. I hadn't seen her since she was about nine, and I had been eager to meet her again. By some strange coincidence we got on the subject of boys and dating. Betty has "a steady" at college, and when she talked about him she did something unusual— she blushed! When was the last time any of us saw a teenager blush?

I thought to myself, Betty and her grandma must be a throwback to an earlier time. Then Grandma said, "Betty and I have been reading my love letters together! When Dave died, I began re-reading the letters he wrote me while we were both at different colleges. I had forgotten how passionate his letters were! He was much more reserved in person, and Betty can't believe this was her Grandpa writing!" What an absolutely wonderful idea!

We need not feel helpless to protect our grandchildren from the terrible dangers of life if we were smart enough to have saved old love letters or kept a diary. What better way could there be to send a special message without sermonizing or lecturing? What today's young people need to hear is what was good about the good old days. Betty told me, in breathless wonder, "My grandparents were so much in love they waited until they could get married!" She surely found such an idea quite remarkable. I told her that during World War II many of the couples I knew had to wait for each other for three or more years and never went out with anyone else. Betty was amazed, flabbergasted. "What did they *do?*" she asked. I told her they wrote passionate letters and shared such private thoughts that by the time they were together again they were the best of friends.

Old-fashioned ideas and old-fashioned behavior sound pretty good to young people caught in the maelstrom of impulsive behavior condoned by permissive attitudes when one is too young to deal with the consequences. We need to let our grandchildren know that having to live up to some valuable standards was never a bad idea and is now more important then ever.

When Our Children Try to Become Our Parents

"Wait until I tell you what I did with my mother," an old friend told me excitedly on the phone the other day. I didn't know what to expect. After all, her mother is eighty-seven.

My friend told me she had a brainstorm recently when she stayed overnight at her mother's. "Every time I visit her, I can't stand her guest room," she said. "It's ugly and old-fashioned—awful old stuff. So, the next morning, I tore the place apart, dragged the furniture outside to give away, pulled down the curtains, the bedspread—every movable object—and when my mother came in, shocked, I said, 'Hey, Mom, we're going shopping!' We had such fun, she loved it."

Can you guess my reaction? *I* was shocked, for in modernizing that room, my friend, with I'm sure the best of intentions, robbed her mother of the freedom of consent. Maybe she really *did* love the end result, but I knew I would have been furious if someone had done that to me.

In the past, we usually thought we knew what was

good for our children when they were young. Too often now they are paying us back—they are sure they know what is good for us. Even if they are right, we should let them know we must be asked before decisions are made.

Here's an anecdote that illustrates what I mean. One father told me, "My son is a very successful lawyer. I'm afraid he thinks because I live on a pension and Social Security that I'm not bright anymore. He went out, bought me a big, fancy car—some foreign thing I'd never even heard of. He was so proud, showing me he could afford to buy me such an expensive present.

"I've been driving a Ford for fifty years; I like windows I can roll down myself; I like a radio with three buttons, not twenty-five. I have no use for a big car. What was I to do? I couldn't hurt his feelings, so I didn't say a word."

It seems to me Daddy should have said, "I know you love me and want to please me, and I am proud of your accomplishments, but, at seventy-three, I really can't change my habits and adjust to the new technological wonders. Take the car back or sell it or keep it yourself. Give me a second-hand Ford and a trip to Hawaii instead."

Maybe this discussion is more for your children, but I hope if you are in this situation, you will also feel encouraged to speak up. The more our children love us, the worse the problem. We don't want to discourage their generosity and concern for our well-being. So one way to handle what we see as an invasion of our privacy and freedom of choice is to reminisce.

"Remember when you were eight, and Dad and I bought you that gorgeous, fancy princess doll? You were so angry and disappointed. You shouted, 'I don't have to play with dolls just because I'm a girl! I want an electric train!' "

We all have examples to sweeten our demand to be consulted. If we are honest, it will be hard for our adult children not to get our point.

Listening to Grandchildren

SOME TIME AGO A READER SENT ME A CLIPPING from *The New York Times* (January, 1993). It was of a letter written by a person I consider to be a most beloved colleague, Ashley Montagu, writer, philosopher, psychologist, extraordinary human being. The letter was about the fact that we never—or very rarely—listen to children. We have conferences about them, we write books about them, and we study them, but do we ever include them in our deliberations?

I put the letter in the folder marked "Things to save for future columns," and I never got around to writing about it until yesterday when I visited a friend I hadn't seen for almost twenty years. We were reminiscing about when our children were nursery-school age, and we both laughed, thinking of a time when my husband and I had dinner at Sylvia's house and were involved in an all-consuming conversation when suddenly we were startled by a bloodcurdling howl from one end of the table. Four-year-old Ricky screamed at us venomously, "It's time for you to shut up and let ME talk."

While we were young parents so much of our time was taken up with cooking, cleaning, going to work, entertaining, and attending PTA meetings, and trying to have a few minutes here or there for adult conversation so that, if truth be known, listening to what our kids wanted to tell us was often a very low priority. Or we didn't have the patience to listen while they tried to collect their thoughts; we might say, "Tell me what happened in school today," or, "Did you have a good time at camp?" and before the child could formulate an answer we were shelling peas or answering the phone or taking the laundry out of the dryer. Talking to Sylvia made me realize the reader had sent me a gem of an idea, and I had ignored it too long. Which grownups have the time and enjoy being with children most of all—*grandparents*!

I get a lot of mail bemoaning the fact that grandchildren are so busy with their own lives they don't seem to want to spend much time with Grandma and Grandpa. I'm not a gambling woman but I will bet that "quality time" between grandchildren and grandparents would increase by geometric progression if we asked questions and waited for an answer, focusing all our attention on the answer.

Children are not often used to hearing, "I would really like to hear your opinion." At first they may be suspicious, even shocked, by the question, but it's not hard to get going if we pick a newspaper or magazine article about kids, or ask them if they have heard some news that will affect their lives. Children probably love most of all to tell us what's wrong with the child experts! I can assure you from personal experience that listening pays off in many ways—not the least of which is that they are so often right!

Letting the Apples Fall
from the Trees

A FRIEND OF MINE SAYS SHE CRIES EVERY DAY BE-
cause one son is moving to Canada with his wife and
two children, while another already lives three thousand
miles away. She says of her local daughter, "If Maggie
ever decides to move, I'll die."

Another friend is shocked and depressed because her
fifteen-year-old granddaughter wants to spend the summer going on a hosteling trip to Europe rather than at
Grandma's cottage on a New England lake.

After many years of my life encouraging parents of
young children to begin the process of *letting go*, I find
that many of my contemporaries in their sixties and
seventies are having a terrible time letting go of adult
children and especially grandchildren. It is a challenge
of our age group that we somehow never thought about;
for many parents it seemed quite enough to permit an
eighteen-year-old to go to a distant college, to take a
job thousands of miles away, and to accept the evidence
of full-grown maturity when sons or daughters married
and then became parents themselves.

Getting old is a new kind of vulnerability for many of us; there is that growing sense that time is running out. A friend writes, "I think I'm having the first serious depression of my life. I'm going to go to a famous research clinic for therapy and medication." I later learned that the psychiatrist told her at the end of her first session, "You do not have a serious clinical depression. But you are in a state of mourning." What a smart therapist, to catch on so quickly! Sometimes, as grown children move away with our grandchildren, the sense of loss is greater than any earlier separations. We feel cut off from our own youthful years, and the grandchildren who represent our immortality seem to be leaving us as well.

Once upon a time we were the perfect grandparents: we were probably more permissive than parents; we were the best storytellers; we had the patience to play Monopoly longer; we were the people who knew games to make a child forget his or her troubles when he or she had the flu. Now, suddenly, this gawky twelve-year-old is embarrassed by kisses and hugs, and given the choice of staying with Grandma and Grandpa when there is a Saturday Little League baseball game, there is no question the game among peers wins out. It hurts! The special gift grandparents can give their grandchildren is unconditional love, and when the children who have so enjoyed basking in this glow of love for a number of years are suddenly more entranced by other children and larger adventures, we have to recognize we are expected to make a new adjustment, accept another change in our lives.

I am reminded of my husband's story about the apple

tree. It grows and flowers and eventually there are ripe and juicy apples growing on the tree. If one has tended the tree with love for many years, watched it grow, celebrated its fruitfulness, how hard it is to pick the apples or to let them fall. But if we try to hang on to them, if we don't let them fall, they will rot on the tree.

Changing relationships with children and grandchildren are like the apples on a beautiful tree. The only way to see fulfillment of the purpose of the tree is to allow the fruit to be taken from us.

We Can't Always Tell the Truth

I HAVE A DIFFICULT CHOICE TO MAKE: SHOULD I TELL my daughter that her father and I have lived for a total of (approximately) one hundred and forty-four years, or should I just thank her for being concerned about us?

It has rained for two weeks on Cape Cod, where my husband and I now have a home. I have considered three alternatives: suicide, insanity, or building an Ark. Our daughter called this morning and said, "I hope you aren't going out, there's terrible flooding on Route 28." After we hung up, our first impulse was to laugh indulgently and wonder how she thinks we have managed to stay alive—even raise her—if we don't recognize a flooded road if we see one. I thought I might mention this next time we met, but then I had a second thought: It was such a kind and caring thing for her to have done—why should I ruin it?

I am pretty sure I'm not going to say anything. (She never sees this column. Long ago she gave me permission to write about her as long as she never had to read it.) I won't say anything to her, but Larry and I need to keep our own perspective. We have lived a long time,

managed to function exceedingly well, all things considered, and do know how to stay out of the rain, real-
istically as well as metaphorically. If we have loving,
devoted adult children it is likely that we 1.) don't want
to hurt their feelings and 2.) must not let their infan-
tilizing statements get under our skin. That's not easy,
as many of us have found out, if one or more perfectly
darling children insist on holding us up when we still
know how to walk, or tell us that we should be wearing
a sweater (they sure know how to get back at us!), or
that we can't go to the doctor alone when we have been
doing it since we were about fifteen, or why we can't
possibly have pizza for dinner—the cholesterol will kill
us—when we think we're still sound enough of body
and mind to make this decision.

Maybe we laugh inwardly, but sooner or later it really
has an insidious brainwashing effect. We begin to wonder if we are senile; we worry that we are on the verge
of collapse. Do our children know something we don't
know? We need to pay attention to these moments of
doubt, and then tell ourselves it's nice to be loved but
they don't know a damned thing about old age. Someday
they will worry when their children get anxious about
them.

I'm not going to say a word, and this is not merely to
avoid hurting my daughter's feelings. Sometime in the
future she may be assessing my condition correctly and
then I'll be *glad* she wants to take care of me. There's
just no hurry.

Mothers and Daughters

IF MEMORY SERVES ME (AND OFTEN IT DOESN'T), it seems to me that when I and my friends were mothers of teen-agers, most of the bloodiest battles involved our daughters and most of the pride and devotion had to do with our sons. When we mothers met we were inclined to admit (only in whispers) that we wished we had more sons and fewer daughters.

Now, at an advanced age, I sure am glad that one of my closest friends is my daughter. Of course there are exceptions, but generally it seems to me that the honeymoon with sons pretty much ends when they leave home and when they marry. One mother tells me, "My son and I have nothing in common anymore." Another says, "All this talk about gaining a daughter when your son marries is mostly wishful thinking." For those of us who thought our daughters would go on hating us as much as they did at thirteen, there is joy in the land. Every year mothers and daughters understand each other better as the age difference tends to diminish.

Not that all is sweetness and light; it seems to me that mother-daughter relations in our later years either become better and better or far worse than a relationship with a son. I think that this happens because whatever else a woman may do with her life, nurturing the young is still a pretty popular activity. This sometimes wonderful, sometimes dreadful task draws women together. How often in parent discussion groups I have heard young mothers, in describing the challenges of child-raising, say, "I'm going to call my mother as soon as I get home and apologize."

When a truly destructive relationship existed in childhood and did not get better, the anger and bitterness of a daughter is worse than when this happens with a son. There is a feeling of terrible betrayal, as if a natural connection has been destroyed. One friend told me, "With Bill, I call him when I need help with my taxes and I buy his wife nice presents and he comes home for Thanksgiving—it's easy and smooth. With my daughter, we compete, we get furious, we both feel hurt half the time, but we are ten times closer than I am with my son."

This is a generalization, but I think more often than not valid; beyond being the same sex, mothers and daughters have developed communication to a fine art—screaming fights followed by the tenderest affection, followed by a feeling that whether they like it or not they are still connected to each other. Something about sharing the special equipment for continuing the human race. The closer the connection, the more capacity for love and hate.

VI

OUTLIVING OUR BODIES

Finding the Right Doctor

Two experiences with the medical profession reminded me of the importance of being ever vigilant in taking responsibility for choosing the medical professionals we feel we can trust.

Of course, I can't judge medical experience and ability; getting several opinions and checking credentials are the necessary detective work in that department. But there are two attitudes (at least) that need to be examined. My first experience had to do with the accident and long hospitalization of my father during which his physician never once asked me how I would be affected by any decisions that were being made. Not my financial resources, not my own age and possible disabilities, not my history of caring for him since my mother's death more than twenty years before. Every decision was discussed with my father—which is as it should be, of course—but there was not the slightest interest or concern for other family members. Rule number one for me is that any medical professional for any problem must be a *family* doctor, whatever his or her specialty, and that anything that happens to one person in the family happens to all the members.

I wrote a column that provided my second rule, disclosing my dental miseries and the emotional trauma of a first denture. I got about forty letters from dentists assuring me this had been an unnecessary procedure—I could have had the glorious benefits of "implants." These proposals from well-meaning but total strangers who knew nothing of my personal history, to say nothing of my relationship with a skilled dentist for forty years, upset me. What this attitude implied was that *there is one best way* to do something, regardless of individual differences. It has always been my goal—more so now than ever—to seek those members of the medical profession who see my "case" as idiosyncratic; I am NOT anyone else and the perfect treatment for five million other people might be completely wrong with my history and special problems (among which are a total lack of tolerance for the slightest pain, which has to be a limiting factor in any choice of treatment!).

Of course, we must choose doctors for their skill, but never on that basis alone. Question number one: "Do you want to know about my family and how others relate to my illness?" And question number two: "Will you and do you see me as a unique individual, and will you be concerned with my history, and *my* knowledge of myself?"

Whenever we have to choose a doctor, our most essential philosophy ought to be that if we have lived sixty-plus years nobody can possibly understand our needs better than we do. When we have trouble, for example, with kitchen equipment and appliances, when we call in a plumber or an electrician, we want them to bring their expertise to the problem but not tell us how or what to cook for dinner, or whom to invite! Personal prerogatives have as much to do with getting well as medical procedures. True healing comes from a genuine partnership.

Saying "No" to the Medical Establishment

IHAVE A FRIEND WHO IS RIDDLED WITH CANCER. There is no way he can live for more than a few more months; it's everywhere. The doctors recently found another site. He is in the hospital having every machine available to assure the doctors they have the new location. They suggest castration and more chemotherapy. This is in no way an unusual story. Because my husband has worked in the cancer field for over forty years I know whereof I speak! Some doctors, bless them, know when to quit, when to refer to a hospice where one can die in dignity and with serenity. But too often patients are pushed into procedures that are hopeless and useless.

Here are some excerpts from a letter I received:

> This is a short review of what happened to an eighty-four-year-old woman who was suspected of having had a stroke: I was dizzy, disoriented, and frightened . . . I was rushed into the cardiac care unit . . . I was stripped of all clothing and every opening in my body was looked into. I felt like a

side of beef on the butcher's block . . . When I couldn't urinate in a glass jar, immediately I was catheterized. I had a proctoscopic examination. Also a high colonic. I had tubes attached all over the place, and monitors above my head. I had a CAT scan. Everybody wanted to take blood samples. My discharge from the hospital stated that my reason for being hospitalized had been "overblown." I figure if I'd really had a stroke, I'd be dead from all that activity.

Nobody could be more grateful for modern medicine and its remarkable armamentarium of equipment, but sometimes it is appropriate for a patient to say, "What are you doing and why?" and, "Enough is enough." Certainly these are reasonable comments from a patient with terminal cancer and an eighty-four-year-old woman who just got a little dizzy and scared.

Respect and gratitude for compassionate and expert care are fine. But what has frequently happened in recent years is that the jargon and the mumbo-jumbo from a doctor in a hurry who has too many patients and too much bureaucratic red tape to see individuals clearly should not make us feel *we* have no judgment, no voice in the matter, no rights. Hospitals are very impressive places. When we are sick we want to get well and often we think that means total reliance on the doctors. We leave home responsible, mature people who have been making our own decisions for many years and become dependent babies afraid of being troublemakers.

Patients who assert their rights to remain part of the team are much more likely to get well. My favorite doctor, Marvin Meitis, M.D., says, "I insist that every patient is a partner and unless we are working together, I am not hopeful of a recovery."

Keep that in mind. You are a person first and a patient second. You can say "No," if you feel you need to. You can insist that you are an expert about yourself. The best of the medical establishment want you to feel that way.

A Fear of Falling

I NEVER DID LIKE *FEAR OF FLYING,* BY ERICA JONG. It is, I think, the antithesis of the book I need now, *Fear of Falling.* The Jong book offered a kind of wild, narcissistic bragging—the impulsiveness of youth. Now I need a book about the awful feelings of vulnerability and danger that come to those of us who are lucky enough to live a long time. Obsessive sexuality may appeal to a younger generation; what I need now is help in staying vertical during the day.

I have fallen too many times in the last few years. In the beginning it was because I was still trying to be as young and vigorous as I once was, able to rush around at high speed. It was also because I was trying to adjust to these damnable "running shoes," which are so much longer than regular shoes of the same size and over which I constantly stumbled. Now the problem is more serious due to some disappointing changes in my old brain. I often feel unbalanced, dizzy, a little spastic. When I fall I don't just stumble—I catapult, which is no help to my arthritic bones. I have become so frightened that I no longer enjoy walking as much as I once did. Traffic scares me. When I am in New York the terrible torn-up streets and gutters represent horrifying hazards. My anxiety is so great that I dream that I am falling, and wake up in a panic. There is a new brotherhood (all right, sisterhood too!) of those of us who walk gingerly with canes and swear at drivers who seem so eager to run us down. The fear of falling is no laughing matter once it takes over.

I try to be philosophical. This is just a new reality that must be adjusted to. Being more careful is surely not the worst tragedy that can befall me. And I ought to remember that my friend, Lillian, was walking perfectly well until she was run over by the front and back wheels of a station wagon driven by an eighty-three-year-old man who had lost his license (and had no insurance) because of failing eyesight. She is the best sport I have ever met, and despite far worse problems than mine handles whatever anxiety she may sometimes experience with great courage. Mrs. Coward, that's me. Every time I step off a high curb I expect I will fold up like an accordion.

What I must do is turn fear of falling into fear of stagnation, fear of lost adventures, fear of self-imposed isolation. All of us need to make a very dramatic choice as we get older and experience new infirmities. Shall we try for safety? Shall I get a walker or a wheelchair? Shall I quit walking? Not on your life; not now, anyway— maybe later. My choice is clear: I can die of fear or live with it. Accept the companionship of anxiety or become a frightened hermit. I will try not to lose my cane, walk carefully and slowly, and continue to be able to look at flowers, feed birds, walk to a theater, visit friends. The alternative is to be postponed. Living fully until I am no longer afraid of falling will have to be my goal until I can no longer stand up!

When the Body Screams, "No! No!"

BY SOME STRANGE COINCIDENCE ALMOST EVERY telephone conversation with friends starts out with comments about how tired we get. Perhaps it has something to do with the fact that, with few exceptions, my friends are as old or older than I am. Of course, we also talk about aches and pains and grief over the deaths that come more frequently to those we love. And, thank goodness, we all still try very hard to lead useful, interesting, and reasonably happy lives.

But I think the problem of increasing fatigue is one that many of us have a real problem with. Before I moved to the country I had to go to the dentist. His office was in the noisiest, most crowded section of the city, but it was not too far from Bloomingdale's and my agent's office. I had been dying to buy my husband a new over-the-shoulder bag and decided this was my golden opportunity. I took a bus to the store and then walked to the dentist, over to the agent, and then to an express bus to take me back to my office in Riverdale. Occasionally, along my route, I felt as if I might have to lie down on the sidewalk for a few minutes. Even with a cane I was dizzy and I hoped no policeperson would think I was drunk. But I persevered. And then I had to stay in bed for the next two days.

Because I always had a great deal of energy, worked at many jobs simultaneously, and was a good manager of time and chores, I find it almost impossible to adjust to being old. As a matter of fact, I don't adjust well at all. I keep going until my body screams, "NO More, NO More!" I try hard to be cheerful about disappointments but it isn't easy. It almost killed me not to go to see the tall ships and the fireworks on the Fourth of July because of crowds and standing. I had to face the fact that such a crowd would do me in—and where could I go to the bathroom? I see fewer plays and movies because I am ready for bed by 9 P.M. Sometimes I order groceries by phone although I hate the higher prices. We travel less than at any time in forty-nine years of marriage. I tried having a dinner party for eight people and concluded I could handle the preparation but not the cleanup, so I'm not likely to try that often.

I think I hate the slowdown more than the various physical incapacities, but if we don't give in to some extent at least, we have to remember we may lose more than we gain by being too stoic. What I have to remember is that because I listen at least most of the time to the changing energy level, I am still able to get up at five o'clock in the morning and write columns, magazine articles, and books. What happens with aging is that we need to make choices and bargain with ourselves to keep some of the essential aspects of life alive and well. Even though my husband adores his new bag and appreciates that I spent a fortune on it, he made me promise that the next time I had to go to the dentist (who has a choice there?) I wouldn't do anything else that day. As a matter of fact I listened to him. I later drove to my new Cape Cod dentist along a quiet road with thousands of daffodils blooming everywhere. Sometimes listening to one's body can have delightful dividends.

The Aftermath of a Stroke

THE FIRST AND I THINK THE MOST NORMAL REAC-
tion to a stroke is DENIAL; it's a necessary stage during
which we have time to collect ourselves to face the crisis.
Some men were changing the windows in my apartment
when it happened to me, and when my daughter called
just after my awareness of what was happening, I told
her, "Don't tell Daddy, but something is wrong with my
left leg and arm. I promise I'll talk to the doctor as soon
as the window men leave." After a brief silence she said,
"Well, Mom, I guess you will have to choose between
your windows and your life. You are having a stroke."
Denial over! Larry came at once, and I spent eight days
in the hospital.

About two weeks later the depression set in. Although
everyone said I would recover, I didn't believe them. I
scared the hell out of husband and daughter by saying,
"Since it happened in my sleep, it might as well have
killed me—I've had a good life, I've lived long enough."
Fortunately we all realized pretty quickly this was a normal reaction (both chemical and psychological) to a serious trauma.

I needed preparation for the next few months' events.
It helps a lot to have a daughter who works with geriatric
stroke patients! She warned me my brain "would be
burping a lot for a while—the poor thing was all shook
up." This image helped me through exhaustion, dizziness, stress, headaches, worrying about falling, memory
loss, and the inability to work at all.

During the next few months I began to have night-
mares. After thirty years of on-again-off-again therapy
I read my dreams very well. I knew my unconscious was
telling me, "Eda, you think you're so smart. Where did
you get the foolish idea you were handling the emotional
consequences of a traumatic event? It is a crisis—get
some help right away."

For anyone, if the depression persists, if the night-
mares come, it is time for counseling. I found a therapist
and began to face my rage and my terror. There was no
way to prepare ahead of time. The stroke re-awakened
old anxieties and neuroses. I felt betrayed by my body—
IT COULD HAVE KILLED ME! How dare it! After the
beginning of recovery it is time to face all the irrational
(and rational) feelings.

And the best part was that looking at this crisis from
the inside made me more aware than I was before it
happened, something that is true whenever we live
through the shadow of death—and struggle to return to
life. Now, more than three years later, I have had to
learn I could not eliminate the fact of the stroke; some
problems are now a permanent part of my life. But I
have learned to compensate, to settle for my reality. I
stay in bed the day after I do too much; I use a cane

when I get dizzy; I ask other people (or use my darling thesaurus) when I can't find or remember the right word. I stay away from noisy restaurants and crowds. I moved to the country, where stress is a dirty word. All told, there are many ways in which I have improved my life. And, of course, the best thing about a stroke is that I don't take any of the joys of life for granted. I see each person I love as a treasure and each good moment of living as a breathtaking gift.

Sometimes I Forget That
I Am "Disabled"

WHEN I HEARD THAT THERE WAS A LAW REFERring to "Americans with disabilities" I didn't crow delightedly over this necessary legislation. Being human and limited in my capacity to fully appreciate other people's problems, my reaction was that this was a very nice law and long overdue, but I didn't really feel very involved.

People like me sometimes need a hard lesson. Having just recently moved to Cape Cod, I looked forward eagerly to swimming at the local YMCA. I figured that in addition to swim classes for tiny little kids (about which I have very serious misgivings), I was sure many of the members would be old ladies like me, for whom this form of exercise is a necessity not a luxury. Much to my surprise I discovered I had two choices: Either I would have to climb down a ladder, which I couldn't do because of arthritic feet, or I could paddle about in the "old people's pool," which was small and kept at 87°. I am, at seventy, one helluva good swimmer. I just can't deal with ladders, and the hot pool was too debilitating and had no room for swimming laps. I got my membership fee back—they were very nice about that—and I found a motel pool with lovely broad steps and a railing.

What do you know—I am one of the disabled! And I was shocked. Unfortunately we imperfect humans often have to experience something ourselves before we get the full significance of a problem. Now that I think about it, I should have been more aware because after a stroke I was mighty glad that street curbs had an area designed for wheelchairs, but which also made me able to walk across a street with more confidence and stability. Now I think that two experiences with disability will make me more sensitive to other people's needs. Progress has surely been made, but we need to be militant watchdogs.

What is even more important is our role as educators of younger people who sometimes sneer and get impatient with a woman struggling to get on a bus or a man unable to open a door without help. There are, of course, wonderful, caring young people. This column has brought me letters from teenagers, along with people in their twenties, thirties, and forties, all showing a wonderful capacity for identifying with older people, but some social agencies that should know better and some impatient young people need our help in understanding our limitations. Not angrily, like the haughty lady I heard saying, "Young man, you are so rude that I wonder whether your parents ever taught you any manners," but instead something like, "Hey, I'd like to tell you how I feel." After we educate ourselves, we ought to try to be educators-at-large. A friend of mine, almost blind, gets on a bus every day to go to work. As she pays her fare she tells the bus driver, "I can't see you too clearly, but I am sure you are a person who will help me get off at Fifty-sixth Street." Sometimes all we have to do is ask.

In Search of the Cowardly Lion

WHEN THE DOCTOR TOLD ME, AFTER A STROKE, that part of my brain was dead forever, I was not greatly comforted by being told the rest of my brain would try to take over. When my husband had a heart attack three years earlier and was told part of his heart was dead but that other arteries would take on the extra work, we shared a similar sense of both relief and anxiety. After I reported to my husband that now I had a dead part of my brain to join the dead part of his heart, I said, "We are two thirds of the 'Wizard of Oz'—the Tin Man and the Scarecrow." "Ah," my husband replied, "now our job is to find the Cowardly Lion to make us brave enough to deal with our infirmities." Such a smart man!

What I have found in my current quest to find the Cowardly Lion is that there is no one road to bravery. It takes more than Bert Lahr's magnificent roar. The first piece of the puzzle has been *acceptance*. There is no way I can go back to a time before the stroke; there is no way I can be younger than I am. Like most stroke victims, I felt mightily depressed for some time, often thinking nothing much would have been lost if, when the stroke occurred in my sleep, I had died. An easy way to go, after a full and exciting and wonderful life. I thought this was quite rational, but my husband called it "Depression" and I got over it and accepted the pleasure of being alive, if slightly damaged.

The second aspect of courage was the ability to change my life: to settle for doing less, to give up some of my very energetic administrative talents (such as running two households impeccably and filing papers quickly), to postpone what was not essential, to rest more often, to be far more aware of the need for a careful diet and exercise *all the time*, including never again having a Mallomar until I am on my deathbed, at which time my daughter assures me she will feed them to me, intravenously if necessary, so I can die happy. Meanwhile ABSTINENCE from almost anything I like is the name of the game.

I have the courage—I hope—to accept the vulnerability, the early indications of my mortality, and to determine not to waste whatever future I have. I finally realized if I'm ever going to try playwriting, something I've always dreamed about doing, it's now or never.

The Cowardly Lion must help me with the hardest task of all—to try to face the reality that few are as lucky as we have been to already have had over forty-nine years of marriage. Chances of us leaving this world together are very slim; for one of us there is desperate loneliness ahead and terrible grief. I try to imagine having that much courage if I ever need it.

And finally, I want to have the courage to use that dead part of my brain to full advantage. I tell people who love to talk on the phone that unfortunately the part of my brain that could endure talking on the phone is now dead and gone. I will never again endure rock-and-roll in a taxi or a restaurant. It hurts my surviving brain. It's a matter of making the most of what's missing. And reminding myself that I have been one of the luckiest people alive because I can still write.

Needles in My Behind

I AM SURE THIS WILL NOT INCREASE YOUR CONFI-
dence in me, but the truth is that I tripped over a metal
flowerbox a few years ago and catapulted onto the corner
of it. I broke one rib, crushed another (the result of
sixty-seven-year-old osteoporosis, the doctor said, on
the second item, adding another kind of crushing blow).

The pain was excruciating as well as being untreatable,
except with a heating pad, painkillers, and an anti-
inflammatory drug, none of which made very much difference. I was told it would take about two months to
recover, and it's never healed entirely. I couldn't go
swimming for a long time, my best source of needed
exercise. I can't lift heavy bags or boxes. Rain hurts. But
the main thing was that for a while I became relatively
helpless. Couldn't lift; couldn't stretch; couldn't go shopping; couldn't carry anything. I wasn't supposed to
travel. I had to stay in bed a lot. I sure couldn't sit at a
typewriter. The loss of independence and autonomy
nearly killed me.

I have a very perceptive neighbor who, after knowing
me for only a couple of weeks, during this disaster said,

"I recognize your type; you have needles in your behind." She was absolutely right. Ordinarily I have a lot of energy and I "run things." When I was younger I was a dynamo and I have had great difficulty slowing down. The patience to give in to pain and to let others take over was unbearable.

For those of us who ordinarily have had a lot of energy and were also excellent managers, independence has been a kind of religion. Getting sick or being unable to function as usual is bad enough; what makes it worse is that after sixty there is also a hidden emotional agenda. We used to know we would always get better when we were young, but now we are not so sure. We used to feel certain we would take up all our regular tasks, and now we know that we are becoming increasingly vulnerable to helplessness every day that we live. It is natural to feel some sense of panic, even when all we might have is a slight case of the flu or a busted rib—or even a bad cold. "AHA!" our unconscious declares. "See, what did I tell you? You will be helpless for the rest of your life and never get better!"

If this feeling remains unconscious it can raise havoc with what might otherwise be a reasonably rapid recovery. Stress doesn't help the process of healing. Better to know why we are frightened, face it, put it in perspective.

Sooner or later I will stop having a pain in my back, at least most of the time; I am able to swim again. I had to learn the necessary art of *giving in* when that was what I had to do, until I recovered. I made lists of all the things that weren't getting done; I ate off dishes (sometimes!) that my husband hadn't washed too well. I told myself that all the dirt would get vacuumed up even after a couple of months of dust balls everywhere. I made notes of things I would write when I could get back to using my typewriter.

Whenever I try to do too much I pay for it with getting worse, again. All of us have to learn that we are not the center of the universe, that being dependent on others is not the end of the world—and that, most important of all, a minor disaster doesn't mean mortality is knocking at the door. If we are wise enough we will also realize that such crisis episodes are a necessary kind of learning so that as we do actually become less independent and even frail, it is possible to be brave and creative. Maybe this is the time for thinking of new skills that take less motion. I sit and look at flowers and ships going by on the Hudson River, and even if I can't write books right now, I love to write letters and I guess I can do that until I drop. *Change* is the terror—and the reality.

The Afternoon Nap

AN OLD FRIEND CAME FOR LUNCH. WE HADN'T seen each other for almost ten years. Most of the conversation during our chicken salad had to do with the infirmities we had accumulated. We eventually got around to news of children and grandchildren, but the over-all theme was that when we knew each other before it was as if it had been in another life. Never once had we spoken about getting old. And it was still a shock.

At two-thirty (maybe she saw my eyes drooping), Peggy said she had to go home—she couldn't manage without an afternoon nap. We both laughed. That was exactly what I had in mind myself. Until two or three years ago I never, ever, slept in the daytime. I also was able to watch any number of television shows without falling asleep. I haven't seen a whole *Murphy Brown* program in two years. I turn on the repeats and either fall asleep immediately or halfway through. I haven't seen the whole program, which I love, to the point of terrible frustration. I deeply resent this new self that can no longer spend a day of vigorous and continual activity from 6 A.M. to 10 at night. And, anyone who calls after 9 P.M. is off my list forever.

Okay, so it makes me mad; furious, in fact. But there is nothing I can do about it—or is there? What I am learning is to be much more selective about the things I want to do in any given day and to rest when I need to. I spend that extra time watching cardinals and purple finches at my birdbath. My social life is cut down to a few close friends. I spend more time trying to write plays. Preparing fancy gourmet meals is a thing of memory; it is better to go swimming. I never could stand long telephone conversations and now I turn on the answering machine and take one of my naps instead. I have given up all lecturing and try to do more writing, which I can do in my bathrobe and slippers and don't have to travel.

When we get to this time when those of us who have always been very active feel as if we are operating under molasses, it does no good to fight the slowing down. It must be a time of essences, searching for what is of crucial importance, and getting rid of all the non-essentials.

Peggy left for her nap, after which she told me she would be going to the hospital where she reads stories to sick children for one hour. After that, it's an early supper and reading in bed. I left the dishes, lay down, turned on *Murphy Brown,* and immediately fell into a deep sleep. I awoke refreshed from my nap and, as usual, was furious to have missed the program. It's a necessary trade-off.

Getting Older Is Just Hilarious

EVERY SO OFTEN I GET A LETTER TELLING ME TO BE funnier. I always wonder just what they have in mind. And then I got a letter from a reader, George Dawson, that cleared up the whole problem. His idea of funny is that unless we see what is hilarious about getting old, we will miss a lot of laughs.

He sent me two long poems, which I will only quote in part, but you will get the idea:

I'm writing to tell you I'm living, I'm not totally dead . . .
But I'm getting completely forgetful, befuddled and weak
*   in my head.*
I've learned to cope with arthritis, to dentures I'm fully
*   resigned.*
I can live with bi-focals, but Lord, do I miss my mind.
. . . Now here I am at the mailbox and my face is totally
*   red,*
For instead of mailing this letter, I opened it instead.

And a second (partial) contribution:

. . . Yes, my eyes are growing dim, yes, my butt's no longer
*   slim,*
Yes, my joints are racked with pain and soon I'll need a
*   walking cane,*

*True, my teeth are coming loose, from too much pie and
chocolate mousse.*
*True, we can't remember sex, I'd rather have {my} pension
checks.*

There were many more very funny lines, but I hope
these make the point that I have never been able to
articulate to those who say, "Be funnier." It's not a matter of telling jokes or funny stories, it's simply a matter
of laughing at our aging selves. In his letter Mr. Dawson
comments that what isn't funny is people who bitterly
try to deny that they are getting old. They can't even
bear the word. "I suppose they never sing 'Ol' Man
River,' " he says.

He is amused, not angry, at the way younger people
view us. He tells of a young woman who, reflecting on
his age, suggested he take only a six-month membership
in a health club. People say he should have gotten the
young woman fired, but he and his wife thought, in only
their late sixties, that it was hilarious.

So now I understand; what is funny is *us*! Mr. Dawson
suggests we stop bemoaning the things that are lost and
concentrate on what we still have; he is living proof that
a great sense of humor makes up for a lot of other things.

What I found extremely amusing today is that I
dropped some papers on the floor, and then dropped
the gadget I use to pick things up. Double jeopardy,
since my knees no longer bend sufficiently. It seemed
a very funny dilemma, solved by getting a chair and
sitting down to pick the damn things up. It's funny because it's reality. No escape from it. Only to laugh.

VII

EMOTIONAL HANG-UPS

Failing Never Ends

IN YOUTHFUL IGNORANCE I ONCE THOUGHT THAT the older and wiser I became, the fewer mistakes I'd make. I was thinking about that naive nonsense one morning, when, once again, I had to remember to use the potholder to hold the teapot while making my morning tea. All over this country—all over the world—there are teapots with handles you can hold without a potholder and I had to buy the wrong kind. I am reminded of this rather insignificant failure every morning, but what happens is that it kicks off all the other failures, major and minor.

What I have learned from sad experience is that I didn't get smarter as I got older. I made mistakes both large and small, irrespective of experience and maturity.

I was surely old enough to have known better when long ago, I turned a charming little cottage on Cape Cod into a monstrous two-story house totally unsuited to my time of life. It still costs us, I hate it, but it wasn't a complete loss since it seems to please my daughter, granddaughter, and son-in-law. Why did it happen? Because of an entirely unrealistic fantasy that I could persuade my husband to leave New York and could spend my declining years with a little theater group on the Cape. As a mistake—as a failure in judgment—it was horrendous, but I learned something important. If I was *that* crazy, maybe I really did need to change my life. I took about ten years to do it, but now I *do* live on Cape Cod.

I suppose that is how we all should deal with what appear to be our failures—use them to learn more about ourselves.

Even this lousy teapot; it tells me every day that I shouldn't go shopping when I'm too tired and that I try to do too many things each day. It reminds me of the shoes I bought and never wear, the dresses I give away, unused, the closet full of ridiculous traveling bags that I hoped would make it easier to travel, despite arthritic hands and feet. I see myself as too often rushing nowhere without sensible purposes or doing things on impulse because that's just the way I am.

Some memories haunt me. Like my garden in the New Jersey house we decided to sell because traffic on Route 80 had become frightening and dangerous. My daughter and my husband told me the people who wanted to buy the house that I had designed myself and loved were not nice; I refused to believe it. They tore up my garden—lilac bushes, maple trees, forsythia, the most exotic and beautiful flowers—and the destruction (it all became gravel for easy care!) is still as painful as the day I found out about it. But the worst failures have been in relationships—missed opportunities to make amends, trusting people who didn't deserve it, leaving some things unsaid that should have been said before someone close died. Mistakes and failures are part of being human, fallible. It's okay to remember them, but not to dwell on them in an obsessive way. What I tell myself is that I chose the right husband, raised a daughter I adore, and have worked successfully in a career mostly devoted to concern for little kids. The balance isn't too bad. To hell with the tea kettle.

Expecting Too Much Is Always Disappointing

W E LONG TO BE PERFECT, TO FIND PERFECTION in others. When we married, a spouse may have promised the moon and the stars, and most of us who loved passionately (and unrealistically!) are inclined to overlook, even deny, the good things a spouse may actually accomplish. The same thing happens in raising children. We have this vague feeling that life owes us only beautiful and brilliant children. Our irrational anger over our child failing a math test or not being invited to the high-school prom is a terrible disservice to educating children about Real Life and giving them a sense of self-worth that includes our human falterings.

The worst example of expecting too much, too soon, or more than we can have is about ourselves. Feelings of worthlessness paralyze us—make it impossible to do our best. We get too caught up in our most precious dreams, the might-have-beens, that can't be fulfilled. We feel betrayed by reality. A sense of well-being, an optimistic outlook, the capacity to take action all depend on setting reasonable goals and expectations. Never give up our dreams, but accept the fact that human frailty, changing conditions, and more careful considerations must change and modify our lives.

When I was a child my mother taught me a lesson about all this. For several weeks we had been planning a family picnic to a wonderful forest preserve. It was spring and the flowers were blooming and we could hardly wait for the day to arrive. Of course it was raining, and my brother and I were devastated. My mother calmly put the checkered tablecloth on the living-room floor, and we had our picnic; we sang songs and played games, drew pictures of flowers—I remember it all as an exceptional day. It is essential for a reasonably happy life to be able to modify one's dreams with creativity and flexibility. The inevitable disappointments and imperfections of people and experiences need to be balanced by unexpected pleasures. A friend told me, "When Jim and I got married, I thought he would know how to balance our checkbook because he was a math major in college. It was a disaster—he just wouldn't do it. On the other hand I never dreamed he'd become a gourmet cook!"

Polish Your Crystal Ball

MY AUNT CAROL IS DEAD; MY UNCLE JIM HAS Alzheimer's disease; my uncle David had a stroke, which has left him unable to speak at all. What I find most tragic about these events is the time that was wasted in these people's lives hating each other. For more years than I care to remember these people never spoke to each other. They were wife, husband, and brother. So strong was their fury that they would have had a knock-out drag-out fight at my mother's funeral if cooler heads had not prevailed. They were my mother's sister, brother-in-law, and brother. Now life has dealt its un-surprising blows of death and misery. Was it worth it?

I don't think so. There were wounds, no doubt about it—behavior that seemed unacceptable, recriminations, loss of all communication. But human vulnerability—mortality itself—has long since intervened and I see the loss of love and connections as worthless, even tragic.

When we get into family strife we need to think not only of the cost at the moment, but of how tawdry the whole thing will seem as illness and death close in on us.

In a city where I was going to give a lecture, a member of the organization was my hostess and chauffeur. She regaled me for many hours about how proud she felt because she had disowned her daughter when the daughter had married a black man. This created problems at Thanksgiving; this woman's two other daughters had condoned and supported the marriage and still saw the family and their niece and nephew. The problem was, who would be invited, Mama or the disowned daughter, to the family gathering. They ended up taking turns. Wasn't this a civilized approach? she asked me. Throwing caution to the winds, I said, "Aside from my shock since I am presumably speaking to a religious organization that espouses tolerance for all, I'm sure your decision will be a wonderful legacy to your grandchildren after you are dead." Fortunately someone else drove me to the airport after the meeting.

We need to keep a crystal ball polished at all times so that we can see into the future and try to imagine the consequences of how we go about settling differences. Sometimes, when we take a self-righteous position ("I am only living up to my own moral values") we may be sacrificing greater ethical principles than the ones we think we are protecting. Which is more important, to make an adult child accept one's most treasured values (and often these represent prejudice more than anything else) or holding on to a connection with tolerance, if not mutual agreement?

Once in a great while there may be no choice. If some serious injustice has been done, if some behavior has been truly unforgivable, a splintering of connections cannot be avoided. But I think there are few situations that serious, and in the long run we lose; sadness, forgiveness, and compassion usually come too late.

The loss of a valued relationship has happened to me three times in my life. I keep wondering what I might have done, would I now behave differently, as the acknowledgment of mortality becomes more real. Two of these people are still alive. I feel sad and helpless. Our separating was, it seemed, inevitable. I think about it a lot. Maybe I will find a way to make a new connection. My crystal ball becomes clearer as I see how little anger and misunderstanding will count after we die.

Getting Too Old to Hang On to Anger

SOMETIMES WE NEED TO RELINQUISH OLD FRIEND-ships if there is a great difference in values or behavior that upsets us too much. I had a friendship that lapsed years ago; our differences seemed very important at the time. We stopped having any contact, having known each other for more than fifty years. She did something that I then viewed as "unforgivable." A few weeks ago, a mutual friend told me that Judy was very ill and had to have major surgery. She and I were growing older and becoming more vulnerable to life's vicissitudes. I was surprised to realize that my self-righteous anger had diminished and that our mutual mortality made it seem foolish not to have some contact. Judy knew very well what wrong I'd felt she'd done, and like so many experiences, this one had receded into a kind of neutrality.

I called Judy, who seemed overjoyed to hear from me. We made a date to meet after she came home from the hospital. What I found was that she still had certain characteristics that bothered me a lot, but that she was also an old, tender, loving friend in many ways as well.

I didn't feel I was sacrificing my ideals by renewing contact, just learning to accommodate the normal ambivalence in any relationship and facing the vulnerability one shares later in life. But something mellowing also happens to us as we begin to face our own mortality, as well as that of others with whom we have had a long history.

Of course there are some attitudes and behavior that cannot be tolerated no matter how close the former relationship may have been. When I mentioned to a friend that Judy was coming to visit me, the friend said, "Well, I suppose in her case you can excuse what she did as something neurotic coming from an unhappy childhood. But I've just ended a relationship with a former colleague who, much to my surprise, has become a violent racist in the last few years. There is no way I can continue a relationship where there is such a serious difference in values."

There are some situations in which we have to take a stand and assert a point of view, but I believe there are some issues that are not quite as serious and where we need not feel so compromised. This is especially true with people we have known and cared for for a long time and with whom we have a common history. In Judy's case, although she still does and says things that bother me, I wanted to know about her children (whom I had watched growing up) and we had a new shared experience: comparing our health problems.

Someday I guess we will talk about what drove us apart, but it's too late for anger as we both quietly discussed our common enemy—aging.

When We Become Magicians

I HATE MAGIC TRICKS. MY HUSBAND ADORES WATCH-
ing a really expert magician. I can't stand it because I
want to know how it works and Larry tells me that's the
wrong attitude. What now shocks me is that even though
I can't stand magic tricks, I have become a magician in
one narrow sphere of expertise. Nobody is more talented than I in making things disappear.

My watch disappeared for three months. I know I left
it on the dresser, but I had to buy a new one. Then I
decided to clear out my underwear drawer and there
was my watch at the bottom. It must have fallen into
the drawer. Finding things is slower than making things
disappear. What I have discovered over the last few years
is that the things I can make disappear are usually the
things I have put away most carefully. I know I will need
these things, and I choose the place where I put them
for logic and safety. The only trouble is that I never
have the slightest idea what my thought process was.
For example, getting ready for a trip to Europe I put
my passport against a small file box on my desk so I
couldn't possibly forget it. Total hysteria set in when it

disappeared four days before departure. My brother, who only has ESP for lost objects, said, "You probably put it inside the file box because you were afraid it might slip down behind your desk." Found! I can make almost anything disappear. Hats, scarves, glasses, gloves, legal papers, keys. Three canes disappeared (left in taxis) in a six-month period. Psychologically speaking, this magic was surely my unconscious wish to never need the damn things again.

I can make my wallet disappear with special éclat. There are so many supermarket counters to leave it on after I've made out a check.

Twice in one year my essential medications (by prescription only) vanished as if by magic when I was on a trip. Whenever my doctor knew I was calling from Alaska or Michigan, he didn't even wait for an explanation, but began checking to see what pharmacy he could call.

Sometimes the disappearance and the reappearance are thankfully of short duration. On a publicity tour in Chicago, waiting to be interviewed, I put a cough drop in my mouth and realized a partial denture was missing. It was noon and traffic was awful. It took me twenty-five minutes to get a cab. I raced up to my hotel room, and an angel chambermaid took one look at me and handed me a glass. Magic! My teeth! That was a long time ago. If I pull that kind of magic today and don't have such good luck, I will have to magically disappear myself until I magically find a fortune to give to the dentist for a new denture.

But there are limits to my magical talents. I have never

lost a person. I have never lost my way home (at least not for more than an hour), and I eventually found my Will—it was perfectly safe in my file cabinet under a collection of articles in a folder on "Death and Dying." My husband assures me that if I'd stop getting hysterical, everything would reappear sooner or later. It works for him, but I do not have the capacity to sit quietly waving my wand. I still hate magic.

The Heavy Burden of Silence

Sitting in a doctor's office, I got into conversation recently with a charming woman who knew I was a writer and our conversation started around issues of getting older. The doctor had an emergency, so we had plenty of time to get acquainted. She was tiny and attractive, and I had no idea how old she was and she sure wasn't about to tell me. I told her I would be seventy in June and was feeling every bit of it. I was spending more time in doctors' offices in the last six months than in the whole five years just before that. She seemed interested, so I didn't hesitate to list my assortment of chronic complaints, which I talk about with friends, who tell me what's wrong with them in a reciprocal arrangement.

My companion seemed to want me to talk about it, and I finally figured out why. She was trying to get up enough courage to tell me, reluctantly, that for the first time in her life (she had to be in her late seventies, or early or middle eighties) she was feeling old sometimes. It was harder to walk any great distance, cold air left her breathless, it seemed to take longer to get things done, and she tired more easily.

After a fairly long admission of human frailty, she said, "Of course I can tell you—a stranger—and someone who deals with older people all the time, but I never would tell anyone else."

After she had finally been called in to see the doctor, I realized how tragic it seemed that this nice lady, who I'm sure had a least a few good friends or relations to whom she could tell her troubles, chose to talk to me instead.

We all know people who drive us nuts by being so preoccupied with themselves and their bodily functions. Then there are the sensible, reasonable people who get some relief and comfort from sharing some of their woes, but who basically go on living full and interesting lives. And then, at the other extreme, are those shy, tentative people who think that others will be too annoyed and that they will lose what companionship they have unless they keep up a cheerful front all the time.

The older we get, the greater the burden of silence. We need to have a few people who care enough about us to allow us to let off steam; there's a limit to how brave and selfless we can be. And if the burdens seem overwhelming and we are afraid of exploiting people, there are professionals who can help us avoid repressing so much of our pain or discomfort that it weakens our ability to deal with our problems.

We need to find a balance between a deadly over-dependence on others and an impossible stoicism which is just too exhausting.

I'm so lucky. When I had a stroke, I wrote about it and got more TLC than I could ever have imagined. On the other hand, I also started to see a psychiatrist who was an expert in dealing with my fear and anger, so that I didn't dump it all on other people. Talking about how we feel is good for our endorphins and our immune system. Keeping everything bottled up looks brave, but it isn't. Bravery is the courage to share one's life with others. It becomes more and more reciprocal.

Two Sisters Reunited

Martha and Lillian are sisters who didn't see each other for more than thirty years. Martha, seven years older, deeply resented the fact that her husband paid so much attention to Lillian after their parents died. He felt she was too fragile and vulnerable, and he became a substitute parent, a role of protector he'd learned as a child. He saw her alone. Martha had a full rich life, two children to raise, a husband to share her life with, and a part-time career in real estate. Lillian had a quiet life, worked for twenty-five years as a clerk in a government office, retired, and was having a wonderful time going to concerts and theater, playing bridge, and inviting nephews and nieces to visit.

Then Martha's husband died and by then the children had moved far away. Martha and Lillian discovered at about the same time that they were surviving longer than most of their friends and were alone most of the time. Then Lillian had a heart attack; Martha had a hip operation.

When Martha's daughter came to visit her mother she called Lillian, knowing the two women were just too

proud—and probably ashamed—to get together after
so many years. Martha's daughter told me, "They were
both so relieved! They needed each other and after all,
they had both loved my father."

It is now four years since the rapprochement. Each
woman has a small apartment within two blocks of the
other. They share a concert series, spent a two-week
vacation together, and take each other to their respective
doctors.

Martha tells her daughter, "You know Lillian and I
never got along, but now we're sick and old and alone,
and we've been sisters for over seventy years even if we
didn't see each other, and that's closer than strangers."
Lillian tells her niece, "Your mother has mellowed over
the years. I guess I have too." It need not be a case of
"Beggars can't be choosers." What it can be is a new
maturity that brings with it more compassion and—perhaps most of all—the new awareness of mortality that
comes with getting older. Who has time for the hurt
feelings, the misunderstandings, the less-than-earth-
shaking problems of youth?

What we find as we get older is that we have a common
history with relatives we have lost contact with. Life
experiences change us; hopefully we become wiser and
less intolerant of differences. A widower in Martha's
building had a heart attack. Martha makes lunch because
his children all work or have children to care for. When
Lillian heard about this, she offered to bake him a cake
without sugar or salt. Among other things, it's nice for
two old ladies to do something helpful for others. When
Lillian brought the cake over, she found out that Victor

loved poetry and she sometimes reads to him. Martha's daughter says, "It's as if my mother and my aunt are both free to take care of a man since he isn't a husband or brother. It sort of makes amends."

Whenever we make a courageous effort to go beyond old patterns and old prejudices, we are more than likely to lead a richer life.

VIII

HARD TIMES

We Need Stuffed Animals

In 1972 WHEN MY MOTHER DIED I WAS TAPING MY TV show, *How Do Your Children Grow?*, in San Francisco, and although I came to New York for the funeral, I had to return to California to finish my work. I was grief-stricken. After our work was done I planned to visit a young niece, and I bought a stuffed baby seal to take for her baby. It was sitting on the bed in my hotel room, and one night when I began to cry I picked it up and rocked back and forth with it in my arms. Sometime later I wrote an article about this experience, saying I finally understood why stuffed animals were so impor-tant to little children. One lovely lady sent me a Pooh that she had made, and just recently a woman wrote to me that the article had made such an impression on her that, as a home economics teacher, she had the children making stuffed animals. Twenty-three years later!

I was very moved by her letter and then realized that now that I am long in the tooth (if I only had more of them!) I understand that older people need stuffed an-imals as much as little kids. We mourn more and fre-quently and need to comfort ourselves. In addition I bought a stuffed seal for myself and kept it under my arthritic arm in bed. Then I got an orange cat that is soft and cuddly, and sleeps with me when my husband is traveling. No messy sandbox, no veterinary expense, but soft and cuddly and strokable!*

If this is regressing to childhood, let's have more of it! When I visited a widowed friend whom I hadn't seen for some time and gave her a big hug, her eyes filled with tears and she said, "God, how I miss being hugged!" Her children live far away and her teen-age grandchildren weren't much for hugging even when they visited. I sent her another "Furry, the Seal." When she had heart surgery she wrote me, "I think Furry has had more to do with my recovery than all the medicines I have to take!"

It's nice if we have friends and relations who satisfy our normal craving for being touched; it's great if we want a living animal and can have one. But short of that I think we should tell our children and grandchildren what we want for our birthday or Christmas is a new cuddly stuffed animal. My granddaughter had about thirty-five of them when she was three and still has most of them at twelve. I think I can get by with fewer, but there are some new ones in my drugstore and even though they are expensive I wouldn't be too surprised if I add to my collection. And I urge anyone visiting someone in a hospital or nursing home to bring a present of a stuffed animal instead of flowers. They last longer and they feel so good.

*That was before I got Peaches, who is worth all those things!

The Importance of Telephone Greetings

I HAVE A FRIEND WHO DRIVES ME RIGHT UP THE wall every time she calls me. She begins every conversation by saying, "How do you feel?" For a long time I didn't understand why this greeting made me so angry, but I think I have figured it out. "How do you feel?" implies (quite correctly!) that chances are something is the matter with me. While I'm trying as hard as I can to continue to function—to write—despite various frailties, her question invites me to shift gears, talk about my ailments, give in and give up. This friend is extraordinarily popular. By starting every conversation with her friends by asking them how they feel I'm sure the majority are delighted. They have been sitting by the phone, hoping someone would call; they have a list of troubles they are dying to talk about. What makes me most angry, I guess, is that once in a while I get caught off guard and get sucked into revealing my tale of woes.

It's not that I don't appreciate the love and compassion behind the question. My friend is a lovely, caring human being. But when she asks how I feel, I find myself weakening in my resolve to go on functioning as fully as I can.

What I try to do when I call people who I know have many problems, both physical and emotional, is to say, "What are you doing?" Then, if a friend wants to share some pain, some loneliness with me, it will come out very quickly. "What am I doing? I'm lying in bed because I feel so dizzy." Or, "I'm soaking my feet, they're killing me!" But far more often the response will be something positive, an indication that the person is trying to rise above the frailties of aging. "I'm writing a long letter to my granddaughter in college, and dammit, I have to use a magnifying glass to see what I'm writing!" Or, "I'm getting ready to go shopping—I seem to have more energy this morning and I want to take advantage of it."

If a friend needs to talk about how he or she is feeling, that will come out sooner or later, and we can be sympathetic. But "What are you doing?" implies we see this person as a functioning human being, still making choices about activities, doing as much as he or she can. I hope I can hardly be accused of not caring about people's feelings—my whole professional life has been concerned with feelings, from babies to the elderly. But I think we need to make a conscious effort to vote for strength and autonomy, to be on the side of *doing*. That word implies action, independence, and purpose.

Of course, there are times when "How do you feel?" is perfectly appropriate. If I'm calling someone in a hospital who has a broken hip or has had bypass surgery, I must show more concern for how the person is feeling. But what I will try to keep in mind is that I should be ready to shift to "What are you doing," as soon as recovery is well on its way.

I've reached the point that when my friend asks, "How do you feel?" I answer, "I'm getting ready to climb Mount Everest," even if I am lying in bed with a terrible backache. My answer makes me feel better—it suggests future possibilities for action, for doing. My friend needs encouragement to think more about doing, too.

The Times I Miss My Mother Most

I WAS LYING IN BED WATCHING AN ABSOLUTELY lovely program on PBS, a tribute to Alan Jay Lerner, who had surely written so many of my most favorite musicals. In the midst of my joy I suddenly burst into tears. I knew at once what it was—my mother couldn't watch the program with me. She died twenty-three years ago, and one of our best and most loving connections had been the music of Broadway in the forties, fifties, and sixties. Whatever struggles there may have been between us in my years of growing up we were never closer than when sitting in a darkening theater, holding hands as the curtain went up. She called it "magic time."

Oh, how desperately I wanted to tell her I missed her and loved her; most of all I wanted to apologize, to make up for all the times I made her unhappy.

It had been hard for me to become my own person; my mother was so strong, so much like me, and needed so much to "help" when it often meant choking me off from discovering my separate identity. In my early thirties I started therapy, and much as she intellectually understood its value, the truth is she saw it as a personal attack. I was young and just going through the first half of therapy, which is often negative; she didn't live long enough to see the emergence of compassion, love, and identification, which comes with the second half of good therapy.

I wept, wondering if she had known I loved her—did I ever let her know how I would miss her, what wonderful gifts she had given me, despite the conflicts? When she was alive we would have talked on the phone before and after the PBS program, singing our favorite songs.

Suddenly I knew what I had to do; I had to write my daughter a letter to leave for her when I die.

Darling Wendy:

Never, for one moment feel guilty because you think I didn't know you loved me. You were a great joy to me, my best friend. During our worst times together, I don't think I ever really thought it wouldn't turn out all right. Never for one minute did I regret the fact that you turned for therapeutic help; it was not an attack—it was your having learned that anger and discord don't negate love. I needed to rebel and I wish it hadn't hurt my mother. Your rebellion did not hurt me. I want you to know I was always proud of your wanting to go beyond me, to fight to be yourself. You too had a strong mother—I'm sure I was also overwhelming.

Don't waste a moment on guilt or regret—I always knew love lay behind the need for growth. There was nothing that you needed to say that I didn't already understand.

Who among us doesn't often feel as if we left too much unsaid, with our parents? Did any of us fully understand the depth of our tie to our parents until they had died? Can we let our children off the hook, so that when they remember us it won't be what I feel: "I'm so sorry, Mom." I don't want my daughter to have that burden. We need to leave letters tucked away, only to be found after our death. Children know we knew there was love, even in the hardest times. I wish I could just miss my mother without feeling there was unfinished business. At least I can free my daughter from such regrets.

I had an aunt who loved poetry. When she died her daughter found several books of poetry with markers on many pages. Each page dealt with ambivalent feelings between mothers and daughters. "She left me the greatest gift of absolution," my cousin told me. I hope my letter will help.

Remembrance of People Past

WHEN MY DAUGHTER WAS GETTING RE-MARRIED she made me feel great by asking me to make a fancy dessert for the dinner party the night before the wedding. It was a dessert I hadn't made for many years because of our increasing consciousness of sugar as an enemy, and this dessert could lead to a diabetic coma if overdone.

I was sure I remembered all the ingredients, but just to make sure I checked my recipe card file. The recipe was on a note pad, with the name Frances DeArmand at the top—soiled, a little yellowed, and my heart gave a sudden extra beat (or so it felt) as I realized how long it was since Frances died and how clear her image is to me, today. She was a close friend of my parents', a colleague of my mother's, and editor of a children's magazine for some time. And a great cook!

I felt overwhelmed by my loss and then suddenly overjoyed that she still lives so clearly in my memory, that my daughter remembers this fabulous dessert, and hopefully will give my card catalogue to my granddaughter. If only Frances could have known she would be at Wendy's wedding!

When we have those moments of being hit by the reality of our mortality, I think it would help a lot to think about how we will be remembered, and what kind of immortality we can have right here on earth among those we love and who love us.

When we think we can't afford a trip with our daughter and her family, I try to remember that events are one way I want to be remembered. Times we risked bankruptcy to be together, to have fun. Pictures are another kind of remembrance and next winter, on cold and gloomy days, I am determined I will put all the picture albums in order with notes.

I'm especially lucky to be a writer, so that I have that additional storehouse of remembered materials, but for those who are not writers I suggest that instead of always phoning to loved ones, write letters or send tapes. Phone calls (whatever the telephone companies may say about togetherness!) cannot be listened to or read after we die. Although it drives me nuts when people bring these remarkable new video cameras to gatherings, because it makes for some self-consciousness, the truth is that it is a wonderful new way of recording who we are. I still don't think it's as good as writing letters to children and grandchildren, but that's because I am an old-fashioned girl. The important thing is to get our recipe cards in order and record our important thoughts and write about our adventures. It's a great antidote to mortality blues.

P.S. I know beyond a shadow of a doubt there will be requests for Frances' sinful dessert. Just don't indulge too often.

Frances DeArmand's Date-Nut Roll

1 box pitted dates
24 marshmallow bits
1 cup pecans
1 box of graham cracker crumbs
1 cup heavy cream (unwhipped)

Chop up dates and nuts. Add cracker crumbs and cream, saving some crumbs for the outside. Mix. Put whole thing on waxed paper, roll into a log. Sprinkle crumbs on top. Roll tightly, in waxed paper, refrigerate for at least one day. Slice when ready to eat. Sherry, brandy or rum, optional. Bowl of whipped cream on side.

A Traumatic Birthday

I WASN'T THE LEAST UPSET ABOUT MY THIRTY-FIFTH birthday, or my fortieth and never understood the *"Sturm und Drang"* of all those peers who went into temporary depressions. But let me confess that seventy really bothered me. It was such a shock. I have spent a lot of time and money, therapeutically, trying to come to terms with the reality of aging and thought I was doing pretty well. But that birthday caused a regression I never expected. This may seem slightly insane, but one of the things that bothered me most is that for many years my best birthday celebration was a carousel ride— my idea of the ultimate playful magic. My seventieth passed without a carousel ride—a stroke several years before left me a dizzy dame and even looking at a carousel spinning around leads to vertigo.

I can hear other voices screaming at me! I know, rationally, there are people in their eighties and nineties and older who are still alive and well and dancing through life. I recently heard about a lady who should be my role model. They gave her a big, wonderful birthday party at her nursing home on her hundredth birthday, and when the party was over and people began to leave, she shouted gaily, "Thank you, see you all next year!"

I did pass this turning point and recovered my senses. But at first I was giving myself permission to wallow in self-pity. Why not? I love life too much not to be devastated by the fact of mortality and the limited number of years ahead. Why not? So many things I used to love to do that I can't anymore. Why not, when I think about a forty-nine-year marriage that won't last forever? I want, I want, I want—more, more, more.

I did think of one thing I would like to do on each future birthday. I want to go to the Central Park Carousel, and watch for sad faces of children who don't have enough money to pay for a ride. My birthday present to myself will be to buy a big roll of tickets and give them away. It occurred to me that in that plan lay the secret to my recovery. It is the message that I just have to *change* some of the things I do, I don't have to give up. I want more of everything, but there have to be some creative changes about what "everything" can be.

If it takes me longer to pull myself together in the morning, if writing is no longer the breeze it was when I was young, I can still work but at a slightly different pace. And I understand quite clearly that if I hate the passage of time it is only because I've surely had a terrific gift of fulfillment in so many ways.

When I was young I used to prepare an Indian dinner for company. It took several days; I made fritters and bread and curry—the works. I haven't "had the energy" for maybe twenty-five years. At seventy I decided to do

it one more time! It was a great success and didn't kill
me, but I did stay in bed the next day, and I don't plan
any more such culinary challenges. But life isn't over
until it's over and on every birthday from now on, and
as long as I can, I'm going to think of doing something
I either used to do and miss, or something I've never
done before.

Re-writing the Address Book

THERE COMES A TIME IN OUR LIVES WHEN WE
finally have to face the fact that our address books are
so unreadable that we have to buy new ones. Ten ad-
dresses have been crossed out for the same person; half
of a couple is crossed out, more and more frequently.
There are names of people we haven't been in touch
with for thirty years; we don't know if they are dead or
alive or where they might be. Some names puzzle us;
we can't even remember who they are.

I finally had to succumb to buying a new address book.
And what I found was that it was not merely a routine
nuisance but some sort of watershed in facing the last
period of my life. I discovered, for example, that I was
closer to the last entries in the book. These were mostly
people I'd met in the last ten or fifteen years, and something about each of us had clicked in a new and different
way.

In some cases, I called the people with the older,
longer ties because I realized we had gotten careless
about how important we were to each other. In other
cases, I didn't include them in my new book. Where I

made the effort to see people from the distant past, I discovered sadly that often now we had nothing to give each other anymore. It seemed to me that reassessment of relationships was a good and necessary thing in the later years of life; it helped me see how I had changed, who I was now.

Of course, the most painful part is facing the names crossed out because of death. A beloved young man, dead at forty from cancer, on the threshold of what I'm sure was a career that would have made him an important person in television—a talkshow host on the side of the angels, who would have known how to entice an audience without resorting to salacious topics. I mourned him all over again—a sharp, piercing, unbearable sense of life's betrayals, of what might have been, for him and his beloved wife and daughters. And then another name crossed out, but his wife's name still there, and my wonder at the courage with which she had gone on living and growing. The men and women I had loved so much, and missed so profoundly, and needed to remember again.

Even though we older ones now live with the deaths of so many contemporaries, I feel glad there have been so many interesting, exciting people in my life, and I have a renewed sense of gratitude that as painful as the goodbyes are, I am glad I am still alive, that there could be new adventures with the more recent entries in my book. I'm glad many of them are younger than I am, and I hope I won't have to say goodbye to them.

Take a look at your address book; you probably need

a new one. And if you buy one you will have a chance to relive your life, see where you have been and where you are going. We don't have to have a "deathbed experience" to have our lives flash before us; we can look at the names in our address books.

The One Impossible Loss

A SIXTY-YEAR-OLD WOMAN TOLD ME THAT SHE had struggled bravely for many years to survive the death of her first husband. Four years later she remarried, and two years after that her second husband had left her. She said, "Too many losses—I can't face it."

Acknowledging her pain, her depression, her feelings of desperation, I still said to her, "But you haven't suffered the only loss that is impossible to survive." She looked startled and angry before, during, and after my explanation, but I still think I was right!

The only impossible loss is of oneself. In fact, there is only one person with whom we share being alive, from birth to death, and that is ourselves. If we don't have that sustained companionship—if we don't feel respect and love for that self, then we are truly bereft and beyond hope.

A young woman told me of the sudden end of a four-year relationship. "I'm wiped out," she said. I suggested this was the perfect opportunity to meet someone new—herself. Most of us go through our lives giving little nurturance, little friendship, and love to this inner companion. Frequently caught up, from infancy on, with pleasing others, finding ways to be liked and loved by others, we starve our own selves—we don't listen to the cries for attention. Denial takes the form of migraines coming from allergies; trouble breathing is from pollution; a deep depression or a sense of the meaninglessness of life is caused by a job one dislikes. All of this may be possibly true to some degree, but it is definitely not the whole story. Most illnesses, both physical and mental (an unnatural separation in the first place), are related to the malnutrition of our souls.

I happen to know a psychotherapist who has an extraordinary record for patients falling in love with someone, often marrying, after many years of unhappy singlehood. I have studied his statistics carefully because I have lived with him for forty-nine years. He tells me that he doesn't understand it fully himself, but thinks the clue is that in each case the client discovered and fell in love with his or her own companion—that wonderful inner resources were discovered and nurtured. As they began to fully appreciate and enjoy their own selves, they became free to live full and fascinating lives even when no one else was around. The more they came to enjoy their own companionship, the more confident and enthusiastic they became, so, lo and behold, others noticed and liked what they saw.

We need to live through the pain of the loss of a loved one—and then, hopefully with time, we need to recognize there is someone waiting in the wings to give us joy in living once again—ourselves.

Taking Risks and Learning How to Walk Alone

DORIS LIVES IN A HOUSE OVERLOOKING THE PACIFIC Ocean, despite the fact that she is terrified of water and doesn't want to swim.

"I love to look at the ocean, but I have deathly fear of swimming," she told me. "Someone threw me in as a child, and I've never recovered from the trauma."

Then Doris told me that she and her husband were alone in the house when her husband told her he wanted a divorce. The marriage had been floundering for many years; she had endured his philandering because she was afraid of being alone.

"As he walked out, without thinking, I went and put on a bathing suit, walked out to the beach, went into the water," she said. "I had been taught how to tread water and realized I could do it. Then, instead of going back to the beach, I went out into the deeper water, struggled, gasped, and found myself swimming. I was shocked and felt triumphant. I swam back to land and have never gone near the water again. It still terrifies me."

I asked Doris if she thought that she might have been considering suicide. "Oh, no," she said. "I am sure I did it to find out if I could survive on my own, and I got the answer: Even under the worst circumstances I could imagine, I found out *I could survive alone.*"

Anyone who has been widowed or divorced, and who has never been alone before, can identify with this challenge. Going into deep water to test one's survival capacities is surely foolhardy, but each bereft person needs to find ways in which to test himself or herself and find inner strengths that have been there all the time but have not been exercised.

The people who tend to collapse most dramatically—have an emotional breakdown or become totally dependent on adult children, friends, and neighbors—are most frequently people who have never had a chance to know their own worth, whose self-esteem has functioned in relation to the person who is gone. The lesson for all of us is to take note of such a state of things long before we face making a life alone. The actions that must be taken after one is alone might well have been taken much earlier. These are some of the ways one might get started.

A divorced woman with grown children told me, "I was paralyzed and terrified for six months. Then I got an advertisement for a theater cruise, something I had always wanted to do, but my ex-husband wasn't the least interested. I was terrified of going alone—and then I discovered some of the nicest people I'd ever met were on the ship."

A widow told me: "A man came to my door and asked

if I would come and work as a volunteer for a congressman. I told him I had never even voted without consulting my husband. I wouldn't let him into my apartment, but I came outside to talk to him. He told me his wife had died two years ago. My children would have killed me, but after a few minutes I invited him in for coffee. I realized you have to take chances or it would be better just to die."

Not foolish chances, but risk-taking seems to me to be the key to learning how to walk alone. We have to choose the risks we take, and it helps if we choose doing something we have always wanted to do.

The sudden swimmer never went into the water again—she had tested herself and that was enough. But the woman who took the cruise had a lovely time and the political volunteers are now married.

The Last Roundup

MANY YEARS AGO I WAS A MEMBER OF A NEW YORK State Education Committee. It was a highlight of my life—I worked with the most wonderful group of people I have ever known. When our committee was cut from the state budget and some of the key educators reached retirement age, we stopped seeing each other and it was a sad blow. Some few years later two of us decided to plan a reunion to be held at the retirement community of three of our group. About fifteen people came, some from considerable distances.

We had a marvelous time! There was some serious talk about what's been happening to little children and families—the things that worry us, the hopes for the future. A lot of time was spent hugging and kissing and reminiscing about the past. The reason I'm telling you all this is that within a year after this happy event, two of the women developed Alzheimer's and two of the men died of heart attacks. One woman had to have a pacemaker, and her husband coincidentally went blind.

None of us were spring chickens when we met. If we had postponed or never had our reunion we could never have had a Last Roundup.

Of course, none of us could have predicted the losses that were to come, but I am so thankful that we made the effort to bring together a group of former colleagues and friends before it was too late. After the age of sixty— actually at any age—we have to keep in mind that if we don't celebrate our lives and each other, it may be too late.

I hope I have learned not to put off important experiences. My husband and I often plan trips we cannot possibly afford if we were sensible; we settle for bread and water if necessary, afterwards. When friends want to visit from some distant place and it happens to be an inconvenient time, I don't say, "No," I try to say, "Fine." I can't be sure there will be another chance, and a time of frenzy seems a small price to pay. I try as hard as I can not to play the waiting game.

I lost some precious people after that reunion. I realize more clearly than ever before that losses and gains are intertwined. Whether or not we can deal with the loss of loved ones depends to a great extent on what we did to make the most of our lives with them while they were alive. What I have now are such precious memories of that weekend—pictures in my mind that warm my heart. I hope I will never wait too long to capture such memories again.

Letting Go of the Past

It WAS THE DAY BEFORE MY FORTY-SIXTH ANNIVER-
sary and my husband was out of town on business. I had
come to the conclusion that it was against his religion
to be at home for birthdays or anniversaries. I kept
thinking I was used to it—there was Greece and Venice
and California and England—but what I found now was
that it seemed to bother me more each year as we got
older. When we were young it was just a temporary
separation. Now it had intimations of mortality—a kind
of temporary widowhood.

I had spent the day cooking, having decided I would
celebrate with close friends—schoolmates I have loved
for more than sixty years. It seemed to be a positive
affirmation of my life, but I quickly discovered why I
haven't had a sit-down-company-dinner for several
years. It was because standing in the kitchen for several
hours on my arthritic feet leaves me too crippled to walk
for a day or two. But I was glad I did it.

I had been thinking about the night *before* our wedding—a pretty neurotic thing to be doing since in my
day weddings really meant something! That too, but the

night before, we were necking in the park next to the main New York City Library and a policeman told us—very kindly—that we shouldn't be in the park at that time of night. I haven't forgotten because in those days we didn't think there was anything to be afraid of, and it seemed so romantic.

While preparing for my dinner party skewering the Holistic Health Kabobs (chicken and vegetables), I had been playing all my favorite musicals; nostalgia rampant from every quarter. When John Raitt sang the song in *Carousel* about having a baby I suddenly wondered how he felt about getting old. How did all those divine people in all those magical musicals feel when it was all over? How had they stood it? Alfred Drake and Gertrude Lawrence, and Ethel Merman and Zero Mostel and Judy Holliday? We have all had some peak experiences in life that we wish we could recapture, but to have been so talented and so rewarded—if *I* hurt for what is gone, how is it for them? The most philosophical and healthy response was given by Beverly Sills, who, when questioned about whether she regretted giving up singing, said: "I've done that already."

My peak experience, professionally, was the three years of television, hosting *How Do Your Children Grow?* The tapes were destroyed thereafter, but I have one or two of them. Now it seems as if it never happened. I want to be young again and start all over—this time *appreciating the moment* as I never did then. "Does anyone ever realize life while they are living it?" Emily asks in *Our Town.* Maybe not at the time, but surely when we get old we remember the golden moments and might be willing to sell our souls to get them back. Fortunately nature doesn't allow us to be so foolish. My anniversary dinner was a triumph of enjoying present possibilities while remembering the past.

Making Painful, Brave Decisions

Helen is seventy-eight years old, and while she has some arthritis, and occasional palpitations and gets tired easily, she's not in too bad shape. She still walks and swims and sees friends. The latter is the problem; the number of friends are dwindling. Hardly a week goes by when some contemporary doesn't get seriously ill or die.

If one lives to seventy-eight it is inevitable that there will be terribly painful goodbyes. The problem is that every time Helen hears about someone she knows going to a hospital, or having a serious illness, or dying, she goes into a chronic depression that can last for many months, accumulating new sources of anguish. Perfectly understandable? Right—and wrong.

Genuine grief and mourning is a necessary way in which we try to accept the inevitable, weep for our losses, experience awful shock, but eventually come back among the living and pursue our lives, despite the deepest of wounds. Not Helen; slowly but surely the vivacious, charming person she once was is disappearing. Her interests have narrowed—she watches an occasional soap opera, but has dropped her newspaper subscription and given her grandson her record collection. Once a gourmet cook, she now lives mostly on canned soups.

Such behavior goes beyond grief and mourning. It is a depth of anger and despair against the exigencies of life that is so deep it moves rapidly into a serious, chronic depression.

At the age of seventy-eight Helen has to make a conscious self-willed decision: Are the illnesses and deaths of her contemporaries going to ruin whatever is left of her own life, or can she surmount this inevitable challenge and live so fully for herself that she adds a certain kind of life to the people she loved who are gone? Nothing is more of a disservice to the elderly than telling them they are too old to have free will. If that were true the lives of older people would be a dismal story, indeed.

What I keep hoping is that Helen will eventually make the choice to live and to honor her dead. A few months ago she told me that she had visited a friend in the hospital who was dying of cancer. The last thing this friend ever said to her was, "People who are dying need someone to hold their hand." Painful as it would surely be, suppose Helen decided to work a half day a week in a hospital or hospice just to hold someone's hand? Wouldn't her friend still live, for her, through such an act?

Helen, long widowed, was married to man who loved the sea. Can she recapture his spirit by taking her daughter and son-in-law on a cruise? One friend who died recently was greatly worried because a grandson had learning disabilities. Could Helen offer to tutor him one afternoon a week—or even better, take him on trips to museums, encourage him to draw, play interesting and challenging games for them both to enjoy, in loving memory of his grandma?

Each of us has this choice no matter how old we are: to curl up and die ahead of schedule, or to keep our late friends and relatives close by fulfilling some of their dreams.

Preparing for the Lonely Years

I HAVE ALWAYS THOUGHT THAT MEN AND WOMEN handle loneliness differently, and nothing brought that to mind so much as a headline: "Bulk of Estate Goes to Teen Who Cares."

The article said that an Ohio widower, in his eighties and childless, had become friends with a seventeen-year-old waitress at the restaurant he frequented. After she left her job, she continued to help him with housework, keeping track of his mail and bills. She became his primary living contact, and when he died he left to her his fortune of $500,000.

A lot of people probably reacted to the story with shock or amusement, but I didn't find it all that surprising. Old age and loneliness often hit men harder than women. Men seem to have trouble making connections and surviving. Years ago, they were taught to be workers and to support a family. Females in my generation were taught to be homemakers and caretakers.

Of course, there are also old women who can't cope. But, at the pool where I swim, old ladies seem to meet in small groups of friends, bring their lunches, and do their water exercises together. Every day, sitting stiffly on the sidelines, there are two or three men with frozen faces, never speaking unless spoken to, almost immobile.

I began noticing those sad faces when I was a teenager. I had a long subway ride (for five cents) to and from school, and I often noticed old men all alone. I would feel sorry for them and was frustrated that there was nothing I could do. They appeared so helpless. Even now I have no clear idea why I reacted this way. I think it may possibly have been because my grandmother was such a doer, so confident, so involved in running a large household and meeting everyone's needs. Grandpa was sweet but helpless, impractical in business, never as articulate as Grandma. I feel now that that was the beginning of my understanding of how men and women handle loneliness.

And that's why I wasn't surprised to read that the old man left his fortune to his seventeen-year-old friend. She must have felt compassion, as I do still, for all the men who are unprepared to care for themselves in later life. Maybe what we need is a national organization to teach men how to do that.

Today, things are different. Be happy when your son jumps up as soon as the baby cries. Be overjoyed when you see your son-in-law doing the laundry, folding it, and putting it away. We are finally learning that skills can be shared by both sexes.

I think the long-term effect of this change in attitude might be that when these young men are old, they will be better able to function in order to survive. They will know where to go to find help. They will be able to cook and do their own laundry. Indeed, I think they will face the helplessness of old age with less pain and stress.

I hope that by the time they're old enough, our sons and grandsons will be able to handle lonely years.

Recovery from Widowhood

My NEIGHBOR'S HUSBAND DIED THIRTY YEARS ago. Sally says, "Not a day goes by when I don't think of him, talk to him." That's not the whole story, however; Sally raised three children alone, had a full-time job, and has a wonderful support system of devoted friends.

No one who has loved a partner ever recovers completely, but in the past few years I have been witness to some thrilling events. Marsha took care of her husband for five years during his struggle with cancer. When he died, she was devastated; she rebuffed friends, wanted to be alone, took a leave of absence from her part-time job, and told me she couldn't stop crying no matter what she tried to do. That was a year ago. I got a letter from her a week ago. She wrote, "I don't know why I feel so good when people and the world are falling apart all around me. Perhaps it is because after all the pain I refuse to expend one more ounce of energy on anything annoying or trivial and now savor what is pleasurable and meaningful to me." She was about to visit a friend for a weekend, was again working, had had a visit from a teen-age grandchild, and reports, "I can't believe it but I'm planting a garden again!"

The reason we have the capacity to recover from disaster is that pain and loss help us to see what is more important in life; with more meaning in what we do, we experience a new energy and zest. In addition, in the process of grieving we take into ourselves the best qualities of the dead partner; we unconsciously struggle to make his or her life more meaningful by what we do.

Being able to express all one's mixed feelings is another part of recovery. Millie confesses after months of feeling helpless and lost, "That old bastard! I'll never forgive him for leaving me!" Anger is a normal part of grief. If it is held inside, it festers; much better to let it out without guilt. Sometimes ventilating one's feelings can be a pain in the neck to a friend. Joanne is a whiner and a crier. Every time we meet she says, "Well, you can't understand anything I feel, you have a husband." I finally told her I wasn't going to shoot him for her benefit. She complains about being lonely, not having enough social life, children who neglect her, and heavy responsibilities she can't handle alone. I like her enough to endure—and also because, despite what she says, she has taken college courses, gotten an excellent job, and is basically a kind and loving person who is mending. Her need to complain is diminishing as she begins to feel competent to handle her life.

Whether or not one recovers depends so much on one's attitudes about life in general. One friend says, coming out of many months of sadness, "Well, I'm still

alive and I don't want to waste it." But another friend
keeps repeating the same phrase over and over again:
"Why me? Why me?" The first friend is recovering; I
doubt the second will ever make it.

Sharing Grief with Children and Grandchildren

I GOT AN INTERESTING LETTER FROM A READER; it had to do with the death of her husband, giving up the house where she had lived for thirty-five years, and moving to a different community. Such multiple traumas and woes often leave us feeling that nobody can comprehend our suffering. In addition to grief we can feel terribly alone.

But in this case the rabbi, who conducted the funeral services for her husband, father, and grandfather, asked all three generations to write down their thoughts about the man who had died, to tell how they felt about him, to recall their unique personal experiences with him. At first the rabbi intended to use these statements for his own understanding of this man in his talk, but the statements were so personal, so moving, that each child, grandchild—even a great-grandchild—spoke for himself—sometimes fumbling, sometimes overcome by tears, but bravely going on.

What happened is that the isolation, often experienced by individuals when a loved one dies, was turned into a group mourning, which, of course, is what a funeral is all about. But this kind of sharing through each person's words and perceptions can add to a sense of connectedness.

One of the most awful things about death is that it can separate people instead of bringing them together. When my mother was four years old her mother died, and she wasn't told until a year later when she overheard someone call her a "half-orphan." In some ways she was crippled for life by thinking her mother had simply left her because she must have been a bad girl. When I was eight, my grandfather died. I adored him. I was not allowed to go to the funeral and did not have a chance to do my grieving until the age of thirty-four, in psychotherapy. I took my three-year-old to the funeral of my grandmother. When I cried she hugged me, and I explained how much she was helping me. In my adult life I went to a funeral where everybody talked about the weather, and how to travel to another city, and the best neighborhood restaurants. I was appalled. The funeral was for my thirty-five-year-old brother-in-law, and my husband also delayed his grief until a therapist could help him deal with it.

Whatever differences there may be in family customs, one thing is certain: Sharing feelings, denying none of the pain, and holding each other close in every way possible is the essence of the healing process. At a funeral I attended some years ago, for a man I did not know very well, his eight-year-old daughter, trembling and tearful, stood up and said, "My daddy had kind fingers when he stroked my hair." I felt I'd known him after all. Words spoken in grief can bind us together.

A Normal Fear That Comes
with Age

CATHERINE, A FRIEND OF MORE THAN FORTY YEARS, wrote me a sad letter about taking care of a chronically ill, blind, and deaf husband. When I first knew them they were a young, adorable couple, and they continued to be misty-eyed about each other well into their sixties, proud of each other's work, often sharing romantic vacations, delighted with children and grandchildren.

Then, gradually, Martin began to experience massive health problems, and Catherine needed a pacemaker and then had to have a hip operation. She wrote, "I can get around again although I am always exhausted, but that is not the worst of it. What kills me every day is to see Martin, a sick, miserable, helpless, constantly whining old man who is terrified of what has happened to him, totally dependent after having been very much the head of the household and a college professor—I want so desperately to remember him the way he was, not what I now face each day."

Such feelings are natural, normal, and occur to every caretaker I have ever spoken to. I had the same feelings

when I visited my aged father and had to face the fact
that the person I knew and loved was hardly there at
all anymore. We would reminisce endlessly, more for
my sake than his—I had a compulsion to re-create who
he once was. He tried hard to remember but I may have
upset him with my longing to remember the handsome,
wise, devoted father he once had been.

I wrote Catherine to try not to repress her feelings,
to let them come whenever she could; to bring out the
albums, put pictures all over the house, re-read love
letters, tell her grandchildren about the early days of
her marriage—and then, feel absolutely confident that
when Martin dies (which she is told is very near) it won't
take long before the current images will pass and she
will be flooded by images of the man she married and
lived with passionately for all but the last seven years.

I got a telephone call from another friend who lived
with the same terror for more than ten years. We met
in the street one day and she said, "Eda, it's a nightmare—only you will understand—I feel sick, disgusted;
Bill drools and throws up and is incontinent—I'll never
remember what he was like when we met, or all the
wonderful happy years!" Emily called some months
later. She told me, "Bill is gone. He died three months
ago. I can't even remember what it's been like. It's as if
it never happened. Mostly I remember times with our
kids—especially camping. He could put up a tent in
twenty minutes, and we ate the fish he caught every day.
What fun we had!"

The mind is a wonderful and mysterious thing. I have
never met a single caretaker who worried about left-

over images or bad memories, who didn't recover and wasn't able to be moved by some marvelous internal magic to go back to the REAL life before the disaster. Inside each person the good memories are just waiting for the right moment to reassert themselves.

Saying Goodbye to a Living Parent

W HEN MY FATHER WAS NINETY-SIX, HE WAS FRAIL, often confused, but still in good health. When I visited him I mentioned that each time I took an express bus from Riverdale into Manhattan, I passed Mount Morris Park and was reminded that I was born in a small private hospital facing the park; I wonder what happened to it and remember it very clearly from two other traumatic events—having my tonsils out and the birth of my brother.

My father looked at me blankly and said, "That's not where you were born." For a few minutes I had a completely irrational reaction; I felt as if I had lost my identity—who could I be if my own father couldn't remember where I was born? What I realized is that when a parent lives to a very old age we may begin saying goodbye before he or she actually dies. The same thing would be true for a parent who has become senile or is the victim of Alzheimer's. We begin the process of separation long before the actual death takes place. The agony of separation goes on for a long time. All my memories of childhood are that I had a wonderful father—gentle, loving, supportive, proud of me. When I saw him in his last years, he was somebody else and my heart broke. By the time he died I had done most of the work of grief and mourning.

A few years earlier he and I used to reminisce endlessly. Because I have had so much psychotherapy I can remember just about everything that ever happened to me from about the age of two or three. When my father and I talked about our life together, it reinforced my sense of my own identity. I took it for granted I would always be able to share my history with him. What I had to learn—and I think it applies to all of us in our closest relationships—is that I was fully responsible for my own memories, my own sense of myself. It is nobody else's job to keep my history alive. My father had forgotten a great deal more than the place of my birth. If I want to have a long view of my life experiences, I have to cultivate it myself. And the good part of it is that the older we get, the more we are likely to remember the past as we slowly forget names and faces, where we put our glasses, or what we did yesterday or this morning. What drives me crazy is to get up from my desk and then not remember what I got up to do. But I think what happens is that the details of life recede so we can concentrate on saying goodbye to parents and others, alive or dead, without ever forgetting who we are.

On Burying a Second Parent

W<small>E BURIED MY FATHER'S ASHES NEXT TO MY</small> mother's under a magnificent red maple, at least forty feet high. It was a tiny young sapling when my father and I bought it twenty-one years ago, when my mother died. As my husband lowered the box into the earth I felt the most profound sadness and loss I have ever experienced in my whole life—not merely for my father—he was ninety-seven and I had already done much of my mourning while he was still alive. What I suddenly felt was a terrible sense of the loss of my life; seventy-one years of family life, of memories of a childhood that were now gone forever with the death of my second parent.

I was flooded with a thousand memories. I felt as if my head would burst—that I could not possibly keep my life just inside my head, that I would explode in some mysterious cosmic way. This must have been one of the most painful moments of my life. How does one take all of one's life up to the point where one is now, and keep it, and hold it, and relive it?

If I wrote a letter to myself asking for help, I hope I

would not scold and say, "You ungrateful wretch! You had so much more than so many other people—what about the children in those terrible parts of the world where crazed adults in their rage are leaving millions of them with no parents? What about people who don't have the wonderful memories you have? What about the fact that you remain surrounded by so much love, so much to be grateful for?"

No, none of this helps me at this existential moment of trying to deal with mortality in my life experience. I am overwhelmed by the tragedy of consciousness and somewhere deep inside I know it will take a long time for me to rediscover the ecstasy of still living, still having a present and indeterminate future. Dimly I perceive watching my granddaughter grow to maturity, of more shared years of love with my husband, of the pride in a companion who is my daughter. But not today—not even tomorrow or next week. What shall I do?

I must let it roll, let it happen, and wait for recovery. And meanwhile share my feelings with others who may be going through similar experiences; let them know none of us are alone in our common humanity.

The Subject We Hate to Talk About: Death

IF I HAD A CHOICE OF HOW I WOULD DIE I WOULD
want someone to bring me a limitless supply of Mal-
lomars, and I would eat them until I went into a diabetic
coma and died quietly, in a state of bliss. That's my way
of making a joke about the most painful subject we have
to face as we get older. Death is always a fact of life—
babies, children, and young men and women die before
they should—but if we live long enough we begin to
be more and more aware of our "life sentence."

When my father, almost ninety-five, was very ill in
the hospital and in great pain, he turned pleadingly to
my husband and said, "Isn't there an easier way to step
out of the realm of life?" Later he didn't believe he ever
said it—by then he was rosy-cheeked, happy, feeling
wonderful, and getting magnificent care. He must surely
have been glad Larry didn't try to answer that question.
But it remains for all of us.

A woman I've admired more than anyone (except
Eleanor Roosevelt) spent her adult life serving people
with a joy that was something we who knew her will

treasure all our lives. When she was in her late seventies, Alice Pollitzer became chairman of the board of one of the most creative programs for young people that I have ever been connected with, the Encampment for Citizenship, and her shining spirit brought together people who thought they hated each other and ended up hugging each other. In her eighties she would offer her seat to "old people" on buses, and she died quietly in her sleep without illness or pain at 102. That to me is the answer to my father's question.

I recently bought a new address and telephone book because the old one had so many names scratched out—husbands and wives, lifetime friends, and relatives who have died. A friend of mine in her seventies told me, "I feel healthy and invincible—and then there is a week when I have to visit four friends in four different hospitals who are all dying. I love them and I am terrified of losing them, but I am also terribly angry that they remind me of my own mortality."

When I first began to write about getting old, I knew that getting old required courage more than anything else. Another friend comments, "Death is simply preposterous!" and I agree. To imagine NOT BEING is beyond imagination.

I know of only one antidote to the anger, the terror, of the inevitable. It is to *live like crazy* every minute we can! A friend of mine has wanted for many years to visit the place in Eastern Europe where his parents were born. His need was profound and very meaningful to him but his doctor said, "You are too old now, you might get sick—it's too strenuous." My friend listened, he didn't go. He died some months later—but with an unfinished longing. The best way to stay alive and healthy as long as possible is to be kind and thoughtful to our immune system, which will work hard for us as long as we don't give up and get too scared to take risks and have adventures.

I don't want to know when I am dying; my husband, always the research man, wants to be alert and to observe the process fully. But until those moments come, we live as hard as we can, doing more, seeing more, and living more than we ever have before.

IX

LOOKING AHEAD

Is Anything Ever Perfect?

A VIOLIN TEACHER WROTE TO ME ASKING FOR SUG-
gestions about getting a book published on teaching the
violin. The philosophy of the book turned me off at
once; it seemed to suggest that "practice could make
perfect."

It set me to wondering if Toscanini would have liked
to have been called perfect; or Isaac Stern or Itzhak
Perlman. Or, for that matter, Frank Lloyd Wright or
Michelangelo, or Shakespeare, Keats, or Einstein.

The magnificence of great artists and scientists is
surely in their talent and accomplishments and hard
work, but I think that what we admire most is the struggle to achieve perfection, knowing full well it can never
be attained. The struggle, the quest, leaves us breathless,
inspired.

When we come to the last quarter of our lives—when
we finally have to acknowledge our mortality, we are
likely to feel very sad, even wildly frustrated, for the
tasks we never started or never completed, for our blind
spots in judging others, for acting too often on impulse
without thinking a matter through. As hard as Larry and

I have worked all of our lives, now we see such flaws, such blemishes, in what we have done. I can't look at my early books and articles anymore because now I could do so much better. Larry's struggle for perfection is worse than mine; I can settle for what I've done, but he struggles for the things he may not have time to even start.

A baby is probably the closest thing to being perfect—but even that adorable creature has no control over its bladder and lower colon. We have seen the most perfect sunsets, but I find myself thinking that that scarlet and black coloration comes from city pollution. Love is the very best thing there is in the human experience—and what a struggle that is, to strive for its fulfillment, but never achieve perfection.

What time we may have left on earth we can still devote to the magnificent dreams of perfection—a perfect day with a grandchild, the perfect trip to Italy, the perfect dinner cooked for old friends. The struggle is what counts. The search for perfection can be a wonderful stimulant for creative energies as long as we never forget it is a journey, not an accomplishment.

Retirement: From or To?

THE RICHARDSONS CAME FOR LUNCH: FRIENDS WE hadn't seen for twenty years since we both moved from place to place. It was obvious from the expression on their faces that they were as relieved as we were to see, at once, we still liked each other and had common interests. Except for one unbridgeable sad area. Helen and Martin had owned and worked together in a very fine women's clothing shop. Martin did the buying, Helen the selling; both loved their work. Without having had any children they could devote themselves to attending fashion shows all over the world, met many designers, and had devoted customers for thirty years. Having some mistaken notion they were getting too old and should retire and "enjoy themselves," they sold the business ten years ago.

During lunch, Larry and I realized we were dealing with two seriously depressed people, in excellent health but with no place to go. When Larry asked Helen what she'd been doing, she replied bitterly, "Who has anything to do?" Martin said sadly he was sorry he gave up tennis ten years ago; if he'd kept it up he could still play.

Martin and Helen spend most of their time traveling, mainly to places they have been to before—because, "I guess we've just about seen everything twice already." We should have told Martin to try tennis again, slowly, carefully. We should have told Helen to get the lead out and do something useful.

We were embarrassed to indicate we were still so busy that we couldn't see straight. They seemed genuinely shocked that we had no plans to retire at seventy-one and seventy-four. Martin tells dirty jokes, which he never did before, and Helen seems to have given up things I remember she enjoyed once, such as cooking and reading and listening to music.

We reminisced about old times and Helen said she hoped it wouldn't be another twenty years, and I thought to myself, it can't be.

After they left, Larry, the family intellectual, recited these lines from a poem by Tennyson about Ulysses when he grew old:

> *"Old age hath yet his honor and his toil;*
> *Death closes all; but something ere the end,*
> *Some work of noble note may yet be done . . ."*

And I told Larry I had just heard about a seventy-eight-year-old woman, with no family left, who was planning to cross from Newfoundland to Europe alone in a sailboat. Some of her friends wondered if she should be placed in a mental hospital, but her answer seemed quite sane to me. "If I die while gloriously happy, would that be so bad? And if I can't do what I want now, when may I start?"

It's a tragedy to retire from something we love unless we are ready to fall in love with something new.

There Can Always Be
New Beginnings

WHEN WE WERE YOUNGER AND FACED ADVERSITY it helped to know we had plenty of years ahead to recoup any losses. Some experiences were of course extremely painful—the loss of a job, a miscarriage, a divorce—but even at such times there was the hope—the knowledge—that there was time to find one's way back.

That gets harder and harder as we get older. We begin to have the feeling we won't have time for new beginnings. NOT SO! Even in the face of a limited lifetime, changes, new experiences, and new pleasures can spring forth, often unexpectedly. When a beloved aunt of mine seemed to be dying and my husband was at her bedside holding her hand, he said, "Lillie, it's all right if you want to let go." She replied, weakly, breathlessly, "Larry, there's always another sunset." And she rallied to have more sunsets, more days with friends, and more times to feel surrounded by love.

I had decided that I was about to give my last lecture. Notes about it were the last in my file, "Future Speeches." As I took the file out of my file drawer, I had a momentary feeling of sadness and ambivalence. I have been an educator and a counselor with parents and children for more than half my lifetime; I must have given several thousand lectures, but I had known for some time that the stress was now too much for me. Giving this up made me feel old and pessimistic about the future. During the same week a magazine and I came to a parting of the ways; I planned to quit, but they fired me first! We just weren't right for each other, but another sense of loss had been created. My attitude was, it's too late for new beginnings, I haven't enough years ahead for new career activities or new adventures.

The first thing that happened is that my husband was asked to give a number of lectures and seminars in California, earning enough to pay for a boat trip to Alaska, which was a glorious experience. The second thing that happened was a call from Shari Lewis, the "mother" of the puppet Lambchop, asking if I would serve as an advisor on a new television series she was planning for young children. I took the file folder "Future Speeches," crossed that out, and wrote in "Shari." At sixty-nine I was going to have just the kind of fun I was still capable of having. A new beginning, more adventures. That ended a year later, but since that time I've written several plays, moved to the country, and seen three kinds of birds I'd never seen before.

I have always been a lucky devil, having met wonderful people, and working hard enough along with my husband so that at many times we have been able to indulge in trips. Life has been creative and adventurous. All that is true, but I think the lesson of my new be-

ginnings can be part of anyone's life until the moment
of dying.

One man I know had a better relationship with his
granddaughter during his last eight weeks in the hospital.
"For the first time we could really talk to each other
and I think I helped her with some problems," he reported triumphantly. A woman who had secretly longed
to be a dancer was introduced to a famous ballerina
several months before she died, and said, "Never in my
life did I think I would ever *talk* to a real dancer! It's
the most wonderful thing that has ever happened to me!"
A teacher who suffered a severe depression when forced
to retire because of two hip replacements now teaches
children with learning problems in her home. She says,
"*This* is the size class I always dreamed about!" I don't
give lectures anymore, but one of my plays is on tape
and is being used at many conferences.

Never doubt there can still be a new adventure in
your future! Just be ready.

Nobody Has to Die—As Long as Memories and Good Works Endure

I PERSONALLY DO NOT BELIEVE IN EITHER HEAVEN or hell in literal terms, but I know, beyond a shadow of a doubt that there is an afterlife for those who are remembered for their good works.

Of course the most obvious immortality lies in the memories we share with our children and grandchildren. From the ages of four to seven, children love to hear stories about when we were their age. Then from about eight to twenty, hearing about us and the family past are not a high priority in the lives of young people— they are too busy (and rightly) trying to separate themselves from parents and move toward independence. And then, as grownups, it is safe to return to the family and there begins a gratifying curiosity about "roots." There are a number of exceptions, of course, where, in order to build a sense of unique identity, especially for groups who need the nourishment of special pride, there never is a lapse of interest, and where memories of us as parents and grandparents may go on, generation after generation. If we want never to die, we need to work hard so that memories of us will be full of loving and caring, understanding, and encouragement.

I have a beautiful photograph of my parents, looking at each other, a few weeks before their marriage. I have snapshots of their honeymoon and a thousand pictures of my childhood with them. My memories are clear— much clearer than my present. My daughter has her memories, and we share these with my granddaughter.

But there are other forms of immortality. I know, for example, that the books I've written, the direct contacts with parents and children—maybe even some newspaper columns—have influenced many people. If only one person had told me I'd been of help in some way, I would treasure that instant, and because I've been so lucky, I have a profound sense of having thrown some useful pebbles into the lake of life, and the ripples have spread beyond my even knowing.

If I send a check to Greenpeace, I know some part of me is helping to save the natural world; if I send money for prison reform, I know I might have saved one crippled soul; if I join a protest march for something I believe in, if I vote in every election, I am one more person who has made a difference.

People who bring hot lunches to the poor and aged are immortal. People who open their own vulnerable hearts to help others at an AA meeting are immortal. A volunteer in a children's ward who brings comfort to a frightened child in pain is immortal.

Immortality is compassion, concern, and love for others. It is giving the best of oneself to others and thereby bringing out what is best in them.

Many years ago I was watching a television program about a group of young men who had grown up in poverty in a New York ghetto and now had become quite successful. They were being asked what had made the difference in their lives, and one young man, whom I recognized, said, "In the midst of all the violence I went to a nursery school where someone helped me to really feel good about myself, really showed me love. It got me off to a good start." That young man was one of my children when I was a nursery school teacher in Harlem. He made me immortal.

You never know whom you will touch, inspire, and help to grow strong. But living in such a way that you care for every child and every person and do what you can to make their lives better makes you immortal.

When my husband and I started an interracial council in a segregated area of the South during World War II, the president of the local NAACP told me, "You will have stars in your crown, in heaven." I felt I'd been rewarded enough on earth.

There Are Some Perks in Getting Old

Helen Gurley Brown was on the talk-show circuit with a new book some months ago in which she made it clear that she hated getting old. When I heard her talk about the book I had the impression that it was devoted in large part to trying hard to delay getting older and that she could hardly stand the thought that it's going to happen whether one hates it or not.

The other day, on a shuttle plane between New York and Boston, I got up to go to the bathroom after having a glass of apple juice. When I came out of the bathroom an old lady was waiting to go in. She smiled at me and said, "What goes down has to come out!" We both laughed and as I went back to my seat it occurred to me that two younger women, also total strangers, would have been unlikely to share such an exchange. Being old has given so many of us a chance to speak our minds more easily, to behave eccentrically—to be our true selves, perhaps for the first time in our lives.

The other day I was in a men's shop with my husband, who was buying some jeans. He fell in love with some suspenders—very wide and outrageously colorful. The salesman—really too young to be so wise—said, "If he can't do crazy things now, when will he ever?"

There are surely frightening, unpleasant, painful things that occur in old age. But I feel compensated for these by the greater freedom to say what I think, not to suffer fools gladly, to feel comfortable talking to strangers, to plan my days without having to be responsible for other people—at least most of the time. What I like probably best of all is not having to get dressed-up or wear makeup most of the time. I wear the same old clothes year in and year out—I despise shopping. If I have to get dressed-up I can still be quite presentable, but I have more time for important and pleasant activities than I ever did before. I choose my relationships more critically, and I never seem to feel the need to please anyone except my husband and a few other people I love a lot, but mostly I feel that I am a freer individual than ever before.

With some exceptions. I have a friend who has face lifts, has her hair done at one of the most expensive salons in Manhattan, and buys new very expensive clothes every year. Sometimes we have dinner together or go to a play or an opera. I frequently wear slacks and running shoes (not that I ever run). Once we met at the opera, and she said, "You look like a bag lady!" We have known each other for about sixty years, so she's more like a sister than a friend, and sisters say things like that. I felt a little mortified, but at intermission a very famous couple came up and hugged me. We had met on a TV show and they liked my books; we had become friends. My companion was impressed. She might think I looked like a bag lady, but she was willing to concede I had a very interesting life.

If you and I should ever meet in a public place, I want to assure you I will be clean and have my hair (such as it is) combed. But old age does have special privileges. I even enjoy swearing more colorfully now. Compare what you are like now to how you felt at thirteen. You will get the point. I wish Ms. Brown comforting thoughts like that.

Seventy-One and All Is Well

A FEW DAYS BEFORE MY SEVENTY-FIRST BIRTHDAY, Larry and I took a walk on one of our favorite beaches. We were rushing the season a little—it was early for this: windy and chilly despite a blue sky and bright sunshine. I was wearing a light sweater while Larry had on a heavy jacket, so the wind bothered me sooner and I turned back before he did. With the wind now at my back I could walk more easily and continued on to a jetty, where I looked to see where Larry was. He was walking towards me, very slowly, using his cane, obviously tired, and I could see he wasn't doing too well.

The shock of seeing this tired old man was more than I could bear. Larry grew up in Far Rockaway, a beach community on Long Island where he was master of the ocean. When we first met he was six foot four, very slim, with a wild shock of thick black hair, and when he walked on a beach he strode like a giant. I used to watch him, fascinated by his straight back, his powerful stride. Who was this old man coming towards me? I know that deep within him there was still that young man. I wanted to weep for his loss and mine. And then, as I kept walking,

I realized I had the strength to live with this pain; the only important thing was that, old or young, we were still alive and in love.

When I waited and he caught up with me, we walked more slowly back towards our car. I noticed that the rocks on the jetty were beautiful, full of marvelous variations in color and texture. I had never noticed this before. I picked up some shells, no longer casually, but looking at them with a new intensity and appreciation. We might have to face old age, but I had become much more in tune with, much more sensitive to, the beauty around me. When we got home I began to prepare dinner for one guest. I had thought of inviting others and then decided it would be more work than I felt like doing. I concocted a facsimile of a gourmet dish I used to make from scratch, by using a few cans and drowning the "Coquille Saint-Jacques" in enough sherry to disguise the fact that it had been made in ten minutes instead of an hour.

I then decided this book needed some closing message. I sit at my desk using a twenty- or thirty-year-old typewriter, having never let any smart-aleck talk me into a word processor; I'm proud of my independence. I'm looking out at a birdbath and two birdfeeders, surrounded by forsythia, azaleas, jonquils, and tulips. It is my first spring living on Cape Cod, a life-change that took enormous courage and very hard work. I am in the cocoon I need for the rest of my life, and I did it against all odds—financial and psychological.

A small white butterfly just flew past my glass wall, and I think that maybe I can live long enough to see the magnificent butterflies of my childhood come back. My gorgeous adorable cat, Peaches, is lying on my feet. Our granddaughter is out riding the horse we gave her, and Larry, just back from the stable, where he saw her take a lesson, says she is improving every day and loving it. The past, the present, and the future blend into all my days. Today I truly feel young in my aging body.

Springtime for Peaches

When I moved to Cape Cod everyone told me that if I was staying in north country, the Cape was a good choice because it didn't get terribly cold and there was very little snow. At this moment there are about thirty inches of snow covering every formerly recognizable object (cars, garbage cans, bushes, etc.). My husband has been trying to get here from New York City for a week; I think he might make it by July. Like everyone on the East Coast we have had little else on our minds but the white stuff—beautiful to look at, impossible to deal with.

My cat, Peaches, races around the house hysterically part of the time and lies still in a state of total depression, clinging to me, at night. Peaches is a very big, fat cat, and when he lies on my stomach, I suffer from sciatica; I get up at least twice a night to change ice packs; Peaches waits impatiently to pounce on me as soon as I return. I'm too much of a cat idiot to just lock him out of the bedroom. I am incapable of doing anything to Peaches that I wouldn't do to a human child. (My daughter has occasionally implied that I love Peaches more than I loved her.)

In the course of this enforced isolation, Peaches has been doing something that seemed very strange to me. He goes to the door (what used to be a way out, now three feet deep in snow on the outside) and meows to get out. I try to open the door and push the layers of snow away, while Peaches puts out one tentative paw and comes back in. This game mystified me as it was repeated hourly until my husband explained it to me. Larry told me that the writer Robert Heinlein has explained this behavior among cats. They believe that if they repeatedly come to a door they will eventually find the springtime. It makes perfect sense. I have tried to join Peaches's fantasy; together we open the door in common search for spring.

It is, after all, the only way to live through a winter like the one we have had. It is necessary not to give up hope, to keep the image of flowers blooming, birds chirping, temperatures always above freezing, in order to endure the winter. It has occurred to me the same thing is true for getting old, the winter of our lives. It is so easy to feel all the good times have passed, the sense of precious youth gone, and just the new aches and pains are here to stay—it is, as one friend told me (he was only forty-eight—a real sicky) "all downhill to the cemetery." How wrong he turned out to be. He's now retired, lives in a warm climate, and is having a fine time at seventy-three. When winter comes, literally or figuratively, there is only one way to deal with it—an optimistic, never-ending search for spring. Renewed joy in seeing a new grandchild, digging once again to plant "real" tomatoes, hanging out talking to neighbors after months indoors, and feeling the sun on those arthritic joints. Peaches has taught me not to accept a winter of the soul at any age. The insistence on opening the door, this fundamental optimism, makes the winter endurable.

We need to keep opening the door every day of our lives. Peaches is right. No matter how bleak this moment may be, the search for spring is spring itself.

About the Author

EDA LeSHAN, NOTED AUTHOR OF MORE THAN twenty-six books, including *It's Better to Be Over the Hill Than Under It: Thoughts on Life Over Sixty*, *Grandparenting in a Changing World*, and *When Your Child Drives You Crazy*, holds a master's degree in child psychology, and has been an educator and family counselor for more than forty-five years. She writes a weekly syndicated column for *Newsday*, and has contributed to *Woman's Day*, *Parents*, and other national magazines. She lives in New York City and Cape Cod, Massachusetts.